Rambling On

Also by Mike Harding

THE 14½lb BUDGIE

THE UNLUCKIEST MAN IN THE WORLD AND SIMILAR
DISASTERS

THE ARMCHAIR ANARCHIST'S ALMANAC

KILLER BUDGIES

WHEN THE MARTIANS LAND IN HUDDERSFIELD

YOU CAN SEE THE ANGEL'S BUM, MISS WORSWICK!

for children
BARNABY BARNABY BOY WONDER

MIKE HARDING

Rambling On

An Encyclopaedic Look at
The World of Perambulation

Illustrations by *Larry*

GUILD PUBLISHING LONDON

This edition published 1986 by Book Club Associates by arrangement with Robson Books Ltd.

Text copyright © 1986 Mike Harding
Illustrations copyright © 1986 Larry

British Library Cataloguing in Publication Data

Harding, Mike
  Rambling On.
  1. Walking—Anecdotes, facetiae, satire, etc.
  I. Title
  796.5'1   GV199.5

ISBN 0-86051-389-0

Typesetting and origination by:
Grainger Photosetting Ltd., Southend-on-Sea, Essex.
Printed in Great Britain by St. Edmunsbury Press Ltd.,
Bury St. Edmunds, Suffolk.
Bound by Dorstel Press Ltd., Harlow, Essex.

Contents

FOREWARNED

Rambling is a pastime of such ancient pedigree that
Juvenal in his Satires speaks of:

*Urbs in rus pedestria volent non parve quid non erat in omnibus ad
agris et cum perambulae in rus et chuckus eorum much in terra est.
Civitas Romanus cum quid hairy legs et horribilis est quandam
cohabitam ab tectum stannum pullus domus, pullae terrare est de
mortis et agricolae sunt absolutely sic sic sic in dentus rearus est de
Romanus Civitas cum eorum aspectus sudares et eorum crus
capillus et eorum saccus plenus quid vinum et olea et caseus et
chuckus amphorae in terra ut ita dicem ownus eo sanguinus
pigging gaffus! Idus marchus multum non bona est quandum agris
plenum est cum politicus terrare ex Romanus.*

Which translates very roughly as:
'The people of Rome leave on the buses every Sunday
and walk in the country. The farmers are sick to the back
teeth of the sight of them with their hairy legs and sweaty
faces and rucksacks full of cheese and olives and wine
leaving the bottles tossed around everywhere as though
they own the pigging bloody place! They climb on the tin
roofs of the hen huts and make love on them frightening
the chickens to death. It is particularly bad around the Ides
of March when the countryside is chocka with frightened
rambling politicians.'
Rambling was defined by Dr Johnson as: 'An aimless
peregrination of a rural nature undertaken by men who
are tired of the town yet don't know enough of the
country to hate it.' It was Dr Johnson also who said of
women ramblers: 'One is amazed not that it is done well

but that they should wish to do it at all. It is rather like a chicken desiring to learn to roller skate.'

This may be pure sour grapes on Dr Johnson's part, since it is known that he had undertaken one or two Rambling tours of the highlands and islands of Scotland which he'd detested. In the course of his travels he'd been set upon by rabid ducks, molested by a deranged nun and cheated of forty guineas by a man claiming to be God's brother-in-law. As if that wasn't enough to make any lexicographer chuck in his index, the Hiberian cuisine was far from the London standard that Johnson had been used to; one meal served up to him in the Hebrides he describes as 'Swan's snot in rhubarb sauce.'

It would appear that his memories of his Rambling days were not happy ones, particularly since legend has it that Boswell, his fellow Rambler, spent most of his time trying to get the local girls into the hay or between the bedsheets,

leaving Johnson alone in his bedroom at the B and B with nothing to do but look out at the rain and write rotten things about the Scots.

I suppose most of us have, at one time or another, at country crossroad or at urban railway station, come across bands of earnest folk with rucksacks and knobbly knees, baggy khaki shorts and clumpy boots and thought to ourselves, 'Ah! These good people are either African missionaries on their way out to Basutoland or the remnants of a Hitler Youth Battalion lost in Epping Forest when they parachuted there in 1941.'

In fact, gentle reader, these folk are neither. They are *Ramblers*, honest, bull-fearing townfolk in the main, with a smattering of cured agoraphobics and the percentage of deviants of all kinds among them that one would find in the populace at large.

The purpose of this slim volume is to dispel a few popular myths – and to create a few others – concerning Rambling and to examine Rambling from the viewpoints of History, Geology, Etymology, Epistemology, Phrenology, Tautology and Mythology and to see if there is any money back on the empties.

Chapter One

It is very difficult to define Rambling with any degree of
accuracy. As Winnie the Pooh said, 'It is far easier to tell
you what it is not.'

It is not, for example, *hiking*. Hiking implies a fixed
purpose, an object in view, a goal or aim towards which
the hiker moves. Rambling rarely has such a certitude or
end-point. The destination of a Ramble is often moveable.
A Ramble goes anywhere, while hiking is always to
somewhere. A Ramble is more a walk in a general
direction, while hiking always has this *idée fixe*, as Adolf
Hitler pointed out. Hitler was a hiker, not a Rambler. If

Hitler had been a Rambler he would have ended up going wrong the moment he left Berlin, and would probably have spent the rest of his life wandering from *biergarten* to *gasthaus* in the Black Forest. The course of world history would have been totally different.

Rambling is not *yomping*. Yomping was invented during the Falklands War and simply means putting an eighty-pound pack on your back and walking very quickly across miles of boggy land to kill somebody. It's a sort of homicidal hiking much frowned upon by the YHA who do not like bloodstains on their sheet, sleeping-bags or gangs of hairy men, their faces covered in soot, stomping round the common room with mortars and stun grenades looking for somebody to be nasty to while the rest of the hostellers are showing each other treasured photographs of their worst blisters, swapping bull recognition cigarette cards or playing 'Spot The Angry Farmer' in *Trespassers Weekly*.

Rambling is also not *walking*. Walking is something you do when you take the dog out or when you go to the shops. It is something you do when your car breaks down or when the police invite you to take part in their 'blowing up the balloon with the magic crystals in it' competition. Walking is also something that people do competitively for medals and prizes and national glory in the Olympics – imagine an Olympic category called 'The Twenty-Kilometre Freestyle Ramble' or 'The Four by Five Kilometre Relay Ramble'! The judges would pass through their mature years into old age and senility waiting for the competitors to arrive home. Even worse – a couple would arrive earlier than expected, the bulk of the field would arrive later than expected, and the rest of them would be days late while all of them would demand cheese on toast, tea, toasted teacakes, pork pies and pints of ale as though they were entitled to them as some sort of reward for having finished the course.

No, Rambling is not walking, nor ever will be. Walking is something shopwalkers and streetwalkers do. Rambling may change (dayglo cagoules, for instance, have totally superseded the drab khaki drill of former years, which used to make ramblers in the rain look like mobile giant cow-pats) but I still find it hard to visualize streetwalkers, or 'ladies of easy virtue' as they used to be known, standing beside Lakeland paths or half-way up Snowdon swinging their handbags, Barclaycard machines at the ready, waiting for the rambling equivalent of kerb-crawlers to come · cruising out of the mist and the sleet in their fibrepile jackets and vibram-soled boots.

'Looking for a good time, dearie?'

'You can bugger off, I'm looking for the youth hostel at Capel Currig.'

So, if Rambling is none of these things, then what is it? I could reply, as Humpty Dumpty did to Alice, that it is whatever you want it to be. That would be merely dodging the issue. To put it basically, a Ramble is a gentle meandering sort of walk in the countryside of anything between five miles and thirty; it might go over mountains of three thousand foot or so or, then again, it might stick to the valley bottoms. It might require the assistance of a team of mini-Sherpas and a succession of support camps but, on the other hand, it might be merely a gentle stroll along a river bank and through gently quivering hayfields, requiring nothing other than the ability to outrun the bull while reading a map and a sixth sense that enables you to find the one pub in the sleepy little village that (a) isn't full of yuppies drinking lager and talking about holidays, money, fitted kitchens or cars; (b) hasn't recently been turned into a fun pub with dayglo seat-covers, a fun-fur-covered bar and an Australian barman called Wayne who thinks that beer is something bright yellow, arctic cold and fizzy; and (c) hasn't got a sign up saying 'NO BIKERS, MORRIS DANCERS, RAMBLERS WITH MUDDY BOOTS OR LEPERS, BY ORDER!'

Rambling is the sort of walking that you can do with the kids for a couple of leisurely hours on a Sunday, when your only worry is where to get an ice cream for them before they assassinate you and it's also the sort of walking that might take you from one end of the country to another along mountain ridges where your main worry will be not what to do when the mist comes in but what sort of the seven different varieties of mist it's going to be when it arrives.

Rambling is the sort of walking you can do in a party of ten or twenty, where the sound of lark and curlew is drowned out by chit chat about the effectiveness of axle grease as a skin waterproofing agent and the cost of toasted teacakes in the last village or it can be undertaken on a solitary basis by those who wish to 'Wander lonely as a cloud'. Into this category come the deranged misanthropes who snarl at everybody they meet along the way as though it's their mountain. Mind you, if your name's the Duke of Westmoreland it probably is.

And, finally, Rambling is the sort of walking that can take you a couple of hours or several months to do, whichever takes your fancy. It is the sort of walking that can mean that you're back before anybody knows you're gone, so that they all look up amazedly when you return in muddy boots and sweat-caked shirt with bramble scratches and bull-hoof marks covering every inch of your body, and cry, 'We thought you'd gone to put the kettle on!' And it's also the sort of walking from which you can return after months away and find, like Rip Van Winkle, that everything has changed, the kids don't recognize you, the dog goes for your ankles and a strange man opens the door wearing your dressing gown and asks gruffly, 'Who are you?' or shouts, 'Bugger off and get a job like the rest of us, you're the fifth tramp we've had here today!'

As an afterthought, it has just occurred to me that nowadays, Rambling is always undertaken out of doors and can no longer be classified as an indoor sport. The Victorians did build a few covered Ramblerdromes, but they were never successful since people soon grew tired of walking round in circles getting dizzy and falling over.

So what is Rambling? Well the short answer is that, as Voltaire said, 'Rambling, like a whore, is all things to all men'. I must point out that Voltaire's definition is not the official motto of the Ramblers Association.

A Short Discourse on Crypto Rambling

There are varieties of crypto-Rambling, or pseudo-Rambling, which have ensnared many of the unwary and are to be avoided like the very plague. The first of these is *mass walking*. Mass walking bears as much resemblance to Rambling as canaries do to road drills. Mass walking is usually undertaken for charity and involves hundreds of people, who otherwise would never venture into the country, in exhausting and often dangerous hikes that even the SAS would shirk. These usually result in the death of several of the walkers from hypothermia or desert sickness, while the rest of them swear off what they think is Rambling for life, vowing never to put on a pair of boots again.

The types of walking I've mentioned above such as hiking and yomping, fall into the category of crypto- or pseudo-Rambling. So does another form of ersatz Rambling – the *challenge walk*.

Now, without wanting to sound like one of the Romantic poets, I go walking in the hills for the sheer joy of it. I've no misconceptions about Nature – it's red in tooth and claw and it smells and sticks to your boots – but I do believe that a leisurely ramble through wide open spaces is basically good for the soul of a man (unless it's forced Rambling in Siberia). It seems crazy to me that hundreds of people will pull on boots and anoraks and, wearing badges and numbers like common criminals, will set off on a hundred-mile, overnight hike through the harshest of landscapes in the most abysmal conditions. Off the hills they come hours later, sopping wet and freezing cold, bandy-legged and delirious, steam coming from their boots, eyes like bloodshot pickled onions and tongues like rhubarb sticks, crying for water, liniment and their mothers, and so dehydrated that they are a fire hazard. I see nothing sensible in that sort of carry-on.

Another form of crypto-Rambling that is well and truly sailing under false colours is the *picnic*. The picnic never has been and never will be Rambling. There are even people who picnic from the boot of their car, for heaven's sake! True, there are those who pack up a thermos and a pile of sandwiches and walk a few yards off the road to sit by the side of a stream or pond with hundreds of other such folk munching away on corned dog butties and complaining about the flies, but these are not Ramblers – any more than the folk who drive out to the countryside and sit in their cars reading the Sunday newspapers are Ramblers.

I must confess that there are some things about 'the public at large', as she is called, that I do not understand. One thing I completely fail to understand is what possesses the teams of families that you see picnicking on laybys on the A1 and A12 and A everything else, with gran and the kids and mum and dad sitting round a folding aluminium table on folding aluminium chairs while juggernauts roar past inches away, their slipstream sending the boiled ham flapping off down the hard shoulder like a flock of pink bats, the vibrations causing total lemon meringue collapse and, because of the belching exhaust fumes, everything tasting like a north sea oil-rigger's glove. Yet another thing that I don't understand about Man, the motorist, is why people drive to beautiful places such as Howarth Moor or Wastwater or the wonderful Northumbrian coast to spend all their time there sitting in their cars facing out to sea or towards the lake or moor and after the first glance at the beauty before them they spend the rest of their day in the car, reading the newspaper or sleeping the sleep of the just-about-alive, looking for all the world like murder victims, mouths open, teeth in the ashtray and the radio blaring away.

Can it be that they just don't know what the countryside is for? That they don't realize they can

actually get out and walk around in it? Are they perhaps
closet agoraphobes or are they so conditioned by years of
watching television that they can't look at the world
unless it's got a frame round it and the windscreen thus
becomes their goggle-box?

I believe it's more subtle that that. I have a theory that
these people are actually frightened of leaving the car. To
them it represents both the womb and an umbilical cord
stretching all the way back home. They actually believe,
subconsciously, that if they were to stray from it, it might
de-materialize in the strange moorland air and leave them
stranded in a weird world full of sheep, drystone walls and
wild-haired women screaming, 'Heathcliff Patel, cum
'ere – yer tea's on t'table and yer dad sez 'ee'll give yer
some clog pie if yer don't 'urry up!' – leave them stranded
oh so many miles from Surbiton and Walsall, never to
return.

The last form of crypto-Rambler I want to deal with is
the 'I-like-to-get-out-and-stretch-my-legs-round-the-vil-
lage' Rambler. These people clog up the roads of the
country every Sunday, driving out to villages miles from
their homes where they park the car and wobble around,
festooned with cameras, wallets-akimbo, looking for gift
shops with pokerwork inscriptions such as 'You have to be
mad to work here and it doesn't help', 'Pendle Witches
Rool OK?' and other such subleties. You can see them
most Sundays during the season, leaping out of their cars
and heading eagerly for the nearest gift shop, their eager
fingers fumbling with the clasps of their purses. It must be
something akin to drug addiction, this obsession with
spending money on things in craft shops. What do they do
when they get home with them, these 'Make Your Own
Fun Marzipan Stonehenge!' and 'Grow Your Own Real
Glencoe Massacre Scots Bagpipes' kits? What will that

imitation brass gelding-clamp barometer look like on the wall of a bungalow in Chelmsford? And does cousin Maureen really want those dung beetles, mounted in plastic coasters, for her silver wedding anniversary?

There are other varieties of crypto-Ramblers so closely resembling the real thing that they are almost indistiguishable from the veritable McCoy, so I will include such sub-species as the Tap-room Rambler and the Fantasy Rambler in the next section, which deals with the different types of Rambler you or I might meet on the footpaths and bridleways of the land.

The Bog Standard Rambler

The Bog Standard Rambler is a sort of ordinary, no-nonsense, John or Jane type of person, who enjoys putting a pair of boots on and going for a good walk in beautiful scenery. If you asked them why they did it, they would probably shyly mutter something about fresh air and exercise but this is just a cover-up for the real reason they are out walking. They are playing truant. That simply is the top and bottom of it.

When you're out walking you're not working, there's no boss breathing down your neck, no phones ringing, no washing machine running over and no bills to pay. Rambling appeals to the recalcitrant schoolchild side of our nature. There is a little bit of the Huckleberry Finn in all of us (except politicians who have it removed, together with their sense of humour, by a special operation at a very early age) and it is the Huckleberry Finn in all of us we satisfy when we go Rambling. We put our boots on and step out on the hill and immediately we are that little boy fishing for catfish in the Mississippi, the big river rolling past in all its mystery and glory. We are Mole when he has

thrown away the whitewash brush and run to the river
bank to meet Ratty and have adventures, we are Robinson
Crusoe and Jim Hawkins rolled into one and some of us
after we've been lost long enough are like Pilgrim in the
Slough of Despond or Ben Gunn on Treasure Island, ready
to sell our souls for a bit of bread and cheese and a compass
and map.

Your Bog Standard Rambler wears breeches and
anorak in the winter and shorts in the summer, at all times
he carries a rucksack with compass and whistle. The
compass to find his way and the whistle to blow for help
when he finds that he hasn't found his way. He tends to get
lost a bit, get sunburnt a bit, get frostbite a bit and get
stung and nettled a lot. He pays his taxes and tends on the

whole to be law-abiding (although he has been known occasionally to run very quickly across a field with a No Right of Way sign in it). There's not much more I can say about him – he's your Bog Standard ordinary Rambler, and very dull he is too. Much more interesting are the other more deviant types of Ramblers.

These are, in no particular order, the Gear Freak or Gadget Rambler, the Death or Glory Rambler, the Heath Robinson Rambler, the Strumpet Rambler, the Jonah Rambler. There are also interesting sub-groups, such as Masonic Ramblers, Hare Krishna Ramblers, Zen Ramblers, Tap-Room Ramblers, Hell's Ramblers, Jehovah's Ramblers, Marxist Ramblers, Feminist Ramblers, Right-Wing Ramblers and New Romantic Ramblers.

The Gear Freak or Gadget Rambler

Firstly, let's look at the Gear Freak. He's usually absolutely up to date with everything technology can devise for the walker, pedometers to measure how far he's been, altimeters to measure how high he's been and if someone could devise one I'm sure he'd buy a contentometer to find out if he'd enjoyed it or not.

The Gear Freak has a tent that puts itself up if you just add water to it, and a solar-powered cooking stove that can cook a *cordon bleu* meal for fifty in three and a half minutes and yet packs up into a case the size of a thimble. The trouble is that both these gadgets were devised for the Egyptian Army's desert manoeuvers and the Gear Freak takes them with him on a rambling holiday in Scotland. It rains solidly every day for a fortnight. There is no sun to power his stove so that he has to eat all his food raw. At the end of ten days his face has gone all hairy and he's baying at the moon and chasing motorbikes, while his tent keeps erecting itself spontaneously, blocking roads, getting him blown off mountain paths and causing rutting stags to attack him.

The Gear Freak always has a knife with a seeming infinity of blades that can cope with every occasion and emergency. One blade will help you fillet a whale, another will show you how to find your way by the stars while yet another can pick locks, jack up a car, open tin cans, write letters to Father Christmas for you and dress your cuticles. When he opens it on the first day of his holidays, he usually cuts himself so badly with it that he spends the rest on a life-support machine.

The Gear Freak has a watch that tells you the time in every country in the world, tells you the times of the high tides on the coast of Labrador and when the next full moon will be. It is waterproof, shockproof and proof against static electricity, magnetism, thunder and lightning, famine, death, war, plague and radiation. One day as he is looking at it, it bursts into flames.

The Gear Freak is easy to recognize on the hills: he's usually bent double with the weight of all his gadgets, staggering along with the computerized, personal sweat-catching tray fastened above his eyebrows working overtime. Wherever he goes sheep roll on their backs kicking their legs in the air, laughing hysterically at the sight of him. He provides them with endless fun. He usually meets his end when the central heating in his tent breaks down in a blizzard, or when he suffers sudden blowback as he's using an aerosol spray can of mock turtle soup.

The Death or Glory Rambler

The Death or Glory Rambler is a serious danger to every living being on this planet. He is the hard-man Rambler who usually involves family, friends and poor unfortunates he's just met in the pub on impossible ascents of sheer rock faces or crossings of swollen rivers. Unlike the Jonah's Rambler he can read a map and does know how to find his way in the hills – but he always underestimates the danger of a situation and overestimates his own ability to cope with it. The Death or Glory Rambler (sometimes known as the Butch Macho Rambler) is usually male, approaching forty and in a last attempt at retaining his youth works out his fantasies of climbing Kanchenchunga solo backwards or walking barefoot to the North Pole by dragging his nearest and dearest up Striding Edge in a blizzard. The Death or Glory Rambler is not happy unless every Ramble he undertakes is at least twenty miles long and involves at least three sheer rock faces and a rope swing across a hundred-foot gorge full of crocodiles.

He has read every mountaineering book there is, as well as every book ever printed about people walking naked across the Sahara, carrying two camels on their shoulder or crossing the Himalayas in a tin bath, and sees himself as Captain Oates, Tarzan and Sherpa Tensing rolled into one. (The fact that they're all dead doesn't seem to bother him. If Captain Oates had been a Rambler, by the way, he would have told Captain Scott in true heroic style, 'You bugger off out in the blizzard, Scott! It was your daft idea to come here in the first place.')

He strides across a field full of bulls swinging his bright red dayglo cagoule about his head, shouting to those behind him who are refusing to climb the stile, 'You've just got to show them that you're not frightened of them, that's all.' Bits of him are later recovered from the branches of trees or found stuffed down rabbit holes.

The Death or Glory Rambler sees a red flag flying, and a notice saying 'Army Firing Range Do Not Enter When Flag Is Flying' and regards this as a personal challenge to his manhood. Striding on, he calls back to those behind who are refusing to climb the stile, 'Take no notice, the ranges are way away across the hill!' Bits of him are later recovered from the branches of trees or found stuffed down rabbit holes.

The Death or Glory Rambler comes across a manic farmer with a machine gun, whose gate has just been left open for the fifty-fifth time that day, letting his entire flock of sheep wander yet again on to the railway tracks where they are gradually being turned into instant lamb chops. The Death or Glory Rambler ignores the little notice that says 'Please Close the Gate' and puts two fingers up at the choleric potato-faced man with the gun stood by the cowshed wall. Bits of him *etc., etc.*

The Gourmet Rambler

The Gourmet Rambler can be a real pain in the sit-upon. Gourmet Ramblers know, or claim to know, the best peaks to climb, the best footpaths to walk, the best bed and breakfast places to stay in, or pub or tea-room to eat in and the best views there are to be had anywhere; and all of them are wherever you happen not to be at the time.

You can be standing on the summit of Coniston Old Man on a glorious summer's evening, the westering sun turning the landscape spread before you into something Van Gogh would have given his right ear to have painted,

and the Gourmet Rambler will say in a voice loud enough
to be heard in the tap-room of the Dungeon Ghyll Hotel,
'It's a good sunset, but not what I'd call a great sunset. If
you want my opinion, I don't think *anything* compares with
the sunsets you get from the Cuillin Ridge on Skye. Now,
if you're talking about sunsets, there's the place! We were
there in the winter of fifty-six, Poucher was there at the
time and Wainwright, and Tom Stephenson, of course,
and Don Whillans and Dougal Haston and Joe Brown and
Tom Weir, and they all turned to me and said, "What
d'you think Maurice?" and I just said...'

The Gourmet Rambler then looks round to find himself
alone on a dusky peak, the noise of people hurriedly
descending or being violently sick behind stone outcrops,
his only company.

The Gourmet Rambler catches and prepares his own
frogs' legs and carries a bottle of Beaujolais Nouveau up
Snowdon, and looks down his nose at the Plebeian
Rambler who smothers his egg and chips in brown sauce.
The Gourmet Rambler has been known to carry a coffee-

grinder the whole two hundred and seventy miles of the Pennine Way; he carries bottles of Malvern water with him in his rucksack on a tour of the Lake District when there's gallons of much better stuff running over the rocks beside him. The Gourmet Rambler sends his toasted teacake back if the currants in it don't come from the right area of Spain, and will only drink tea packed by Jabez Clegg and Co. of Goole. He is rapidly running out of places to eat.

The Gourmet Rambler has an Yves St Laurent cagoule, Coq Sportif walking breeches and walks in hand-made footwear made by 'a little firm in Bond St that made the boots for the Everest Expedition'. He is easily recognizable by his outfit and the fact that he usually carries an alpenstock so full of badges of the places that he's been that you can't see the wood, and wears tee-shirts emblazoned with such mottos as 'Ilkley Moor Joint Lancashire-Yorkshire Expedition 1926' or 'Campaign For Real Dubbin'. He would never wear, as would the Hell's Rambler, a tee-shirt with the legend 'Ramblers do it in the mud', for that would be in very bad taste.

You can easily silence a Gourmet Rambler, almost mid-boast. Just ask him in the middle of his rantings if he's ever been kicked in the Quantocks – that usually shuts him up.

The Tap Room Rambler or Bar-Room Mountaineer

Well known in all walking, caving and climbing circles are the types who spend all their time in the bar talking about what they've done, or what they're going to do, and never actually do it. As their time in the bar room wears on, so the tales become more outrageous and the forward plans more unrealistic. What began as a story about a walk to High Cup Nick in the rain ends as a major winter traverse of several Munroes in white-out conditions, while a proposed Ramble in the Brecon Beacons becomes a major two-hundred-mile walk involving overnights and backpacks, taking in every hill in Wales that King Arthur is supposed to be buried under.

The Tap-Room Rambler is easily recognizable by his or her (unless otherwise stated, all hims in this book can be taken to be hers as well) enormous beer-belly and almost unworn boots. He usually has a pewter tankard hanging from his belt and knows every verse of 'The Wild Rover', 'Tom Dooley', 'Kilgarry Mountain', 'The Manchester Rambler', 'Ilkley Moor Baht 'at', 'The Banana Boat Song', 'She'll Be Coming Round The Mountain' and 'Eskimo Nell'. He sings them all, all night, in different sequences and various states of dementia, so that by the end of the night Eskimo Nell is doing rude things to Tom Dooley on the top of Kilgarry Mountain.

The Tap-Room Rambler is usually pretty harmless except that occasionally he starts to believe in his own inventions and sets off one day on one of his expeditions. It takes several mountain rescue teams, a number of cave rescue teams, and a couple of RAF helicopters to get him back home again. Bits of him are found all over the crags or stuffed down rabbit holes *etc., etc.*

The Heath Robinson Rambler

The Heath Robinson Rambler is a bit like the Gear Freak in one way, in that he's obsessed by Things. But where the Gear Freak will spend thousands of pounds buying everything new that comes on the market, the Heath Robinson Rambler makes all his own. He makes his own patent stove from two cocoa tins and an old catheter and stirrup pump he just happened to have hanging about. (One mark of the Heath Robinson Rambler is that, like the Tight Rambler, he never throws anything away.) He

makes his own cagoule from a discarded waterboard official's waterproof coat, knits his own tent and makes his own boots from a pair of old tortoise shells. His rucksack is an ex-Army Catering Corps piping bag with some straps sewn on it and his compass is made from some bits of Meccano and Lego that he found lying about. He's easily recognizable on the hills because he's always wandering round them lost, looking like a mobile scrap yard with a cagoule with the words 'Halifax and Mytholmroyd Water Board' emblazoned across the back. Everywhere he goes, sheep fall down laughing at him. He provides them with endless amusement. If he marries, the Heath Robinson Rambler marries somebody who weaves her own quiche and makes all her own clothes with the wool from a flock of gerbils she grazes in the window-box of her flat. They stagger round the hills together, their home-made clothes falling apart in the wind, like two anorexics that have been struck by lightning.

The 'I-Never-Throw-Anything-Away' (Otherwise Known as 'Tight') Rambler

It is easy to mistake the I-Never-Throw-Anything-Away or Tight Rambler for the Heath Robinson Rambler since, out in the open, they look remarkably similar with their patches and bits of string and wire, their rubber bands and general air of studied disaster. But where the Heath Robinson type has carefully constructed chaos out of order the Tight Rambler is a fully paid-up member of the Campaign for Real Mayhem. He still has the ex-Army rucksack he bought in 1953 when he first walked up Ben Nevis, the boots bought in a sale for three and sixpence in 1955, and the shorts his father looted off a captured German Afrika Korps latrine trench digger in 1945.

31

He is easily recognizable in the hills. From a distance, he looks and sounds like a very badly camouflaged psychedelic hunchback singing some sort of high-pitched nasal madrigal or Buddhist chant. It's only as he draws closer that you realize what you are looking at is a Rambler in the last stages of terminal patching, and that the noises you've been hearing are the groans, squeals and screams coming from his boots. The Tight Rambler saves a lot of money by not buying any new gear; but on a walking tour of the Alps the bottom falls out of his rucksack and all his clothes for a fortnight, together with his wallet, passport and home-made muesli fall down a crevasse in a glacier, never to be seen again. It takes him months and costs him hundreds of pounds to get back home. But he doesn't learn; the next year he buys a pair of Taiwan-made boots, cheap copies of some very expensive but everlasting Italian fell-walking boots. On a six-day Ramble along the South Coast Peninsular Path the boots overheat and explode, catapulting him off the cliff top on to the rocks below. Bits of him are found stuck in seagull's nests and rock-pools.

Hell's Ramblers

Hell's Ramblers are to be seen more in the South of England than they are in the North, and are particularly numerous in the Home Counties. They wear leather and

denim walking gear, which they term their 'originals' and which, as they proudly boast, they never take off. As a consequence their originals are covered in porridge stains, toasted teacake crumbs, grease from pork pies and cow muck from where they've fallen over. Their favourite food is egg sandwiches and their favourite drink, bottled Guinness. Walking downwind of them on a warm day can be a distressing experience. They wear leather cagoules with the name of their particular Rambling Club, such as 'Hell's Angels Leamington Spa Chapter', emblazoned across the back, while their motto is embroidered on everything they wear, including their thermal vests, and is even painted on their Rambling helmets: 'Live to Ramble – Ramble to Die'.

Hell's Ramblers generally keep themselves to themselves, although occasional battles do break out between rival chapters. The most infamous of their many score settlings, which took place in the Cheddar Gorge tea-rooms in 1981, resulted in four people being taken to hospital with migraine, suspected bruising and swallowed whistles. Police, who were called to the scene of the disturbance, found an incredible assortment of weapons which had been used in the fight, including Tupperware sandwich boxes, walking sticks, dubbin-tin lids, crepe bandages, empty liniment tubes and a plaster of Paris model of Baden Powell, which had been stolen from a pub in Bath.

Jehovah's Ramblers

Jehovah's Ramblers stop you on the footpath to read the Bible to you and to give you copies of the *Watchtower*. Do not encourage them by talking to them or listening to them. Tell them you're a Seventh Day Adventist, a Bush

Baptist or a member of one of the obscure American religions such as the Holy Roller Church of Four-Square Snake Handlers, Fire Walkers and Caterpillar Eaters; that should keep them confused long enough for you to leg it as fast as you can in the opposite direction.

Hare Krishna Ramblers

Hare Krishna Ramblers are pretty harmless. They wear saffron yellow lederhosen and cagoules, and sandals with vibram soles or metal climbing cleats on them. They shave their heads, bang gongs and drums and anything else that's hanging loose as they ramble, and instead of singing 'I Love to go A-Wandering' chant 'Hare Krishna, Krishna Hare, Krishna Krishna' as they go. It is quite nice the first time you hear it, but tends to pale a bit on the ten millionth hearing – particularly as there's not much of a storyline.

One problem with the Hare Krishna Ramblers is that they do make a lot of noise when there's a big mob of them. Bulls do not like a lot of noise, particularly when it comes from a gang of bald-headed people in bright yellow clothes banging finger cymbals and tambourines. Bits of them are often found *etc., etc.*

Masonic Ramblers

Masonic Ramblers always walk with one trouser-leg rolled up, giving people they meet along the way funny handshakes. They would be laughable – if it wasn't for the fact that they always get the best rooms at the bed and breakfast place, the best spots on the campsite, gamekeepers never shoot them and one of them was supposed to have been Jack the Ripper.

I'm very suspicious of secret societies (and always have been ever since I refused to join the Black Hand Gang in our street when I was twelve) so I look on Masonic Ramblers with deep suspicion. The trouble is that you never know who is or isn't one. I mean, *I* could be one – and you wouldn't know until you shook my hand. I just shook my own hand and it didn't feel any different to the way it usually feels, so I don't think I am one. But it's still worrying. Hang on a minute, I'll roll my trouser-leg up and have a look . . . No – it's still pale and hairy with a little scar where I fell off my scooter when I was seven, so there you are. I can't be one – I don't think?

Jonah's Ramblers

You know the sort. They jam the rucksack in the automatic doors of the coach on their way out to the country, so that the thermos breaks and all the corned beef sandwiches and ginger nuts and the banana and Kendal mint cake, which should have been lunch for four, end up mashed in a runny sort of paste with the tea. This, of course, they don't discover until they're on top of Great

Gable when the wails of woe and cries of 'Push the dozy bugger off the top!' can be heard for miles.

The Jonah's Rambler is the one who sits on the ants' nest sending the little swines out in a murderous horde, stings at the ready to wreak revenge on everybody within a four-mile radius – but they never sting the bloke who stirred them up.

Never stand near a Jonah's Rambler in a thunderstorm; he won't be struck by lightning but you will – twice.

Never let a Jonah's Rambler lead a Ramble. You may well set off walking somewhere in the Yorkshire Dales, but it's ten to one that the Reykjavik police will have to put you up for the night. Jonah's Ramblers don't get lost, they maroon themselves – they actually go through time warps. I known one Jonah's Rambler who had to call out the mountain rescue team to get him out of his front garden, and whose map reading was so bad that he once followed a crease in a map for two days and ended up walking along the centre reservation of the M6 over Shap, shouting at all the cars and lorries, telling them to get off the footpath.

A short-sighted Jonah's Rambler is just about the greatest disaster you are ever likely to come across. He'll lead you into a bus shelter, sit down and order a pot of tea for four, two toasted teacakes and two portions of buttered spice loaf from the next person who comes in.

The Jonah's Myopic Rambler, as such a character is known, is the one who says to a farmer, 'That's a nice pig you've got there!' when what is on all fours next to him is his wife cleaning the step.

The Jonah's Myopic Rambler gets so lost going through one farmyard he spends years wandering round it, eventually earns squatter's rights on it, and the farmer and his wife become so attached to him that, as he wanders round in circles bumping exhaustedly into the baler and the muck spreader and excusing himself to the cows and the goats, they point him out to friends and neighbours as a conversation piece.

Jonah's Ramblers bring misfortune upon everybody they meet. They have the reverse Midas Touch – everything they touch turns to solid dross. You could send a Jonah's Rambler off to cross a field with twenty experienced Alpine mountaineers; several would break limbs, a good handful would lose control of their senses, and a few of them would never be seen again. You can stand on a mountain with a Jonah's Rambler on a clear midsummer's day, the landscape below you bathed in sunlight, and from nowhere a black clowd will appear and pelt you with hail and sleet.

When you are standing by a Jonah's Rambler your camera never works; if by chance it does, the pictures you get back are always of people you don't know and places you've never been. Your thermos, as you stand beside him, falls apart completely in your hands; your compass needle points West all the time, the print fades off your map before your eyes, and the pea falls out of your whistle. Walk into a tea-room with a Jonah's Rambler and you'll find either that everything's been sold or that it all mysteriously goes off on its way from the kitchen to the table.

Walk into a pub with a Jonah's Rambler and no matter what the time of day the towels go on the pumps, and the dartboard falls off the wall, breaking your foot – and you're lucky to get away with that. As you're being carried out to the ambulance on the stretcher, the roof of the pub falls in and a gas main explodes and the only one to walk out of the wreckage in one piece is the Jonah's Rambler.

The New Romantic Rambler

The New Romantic Rambler grows his hair long so that he looks like Shelley and always carries a notebook with him to record any deep thoughts he might have as he strolls through the land, head held high, eyes on a far distant horizon.

To him all skies are blue, all meadows green, all crags stupendous beetling marble walls, all moons are full and all blossoms fragrant. All farmers are called Hodge, and are all red-faced peasants with a wonderful, homely, rustic turn of phrase and a great wealth of weather lore and country wisdom, always trotting out such aphorisms as:

> *When crows do fly low,*
> *Then wind 'twill blow.*
> *When crows fly back'ards,*
> *They's just 'bowt knackered.*

He's obviously not come across the farmer I once met who thought, 'Bugger off back where yer cum from yer scruffy sod!' was the correct way to address all visitors to the countryside.

The New Romantic Rambler is so engrossed in his mental processes as he strolls along with his head in the air, thinking his poetic thoughts, that he never looks where he's walking and rambles into the pub at the end of his walk with so much muck on his boots that old ladies faint, the cheese on the bar explodes and the landlord's dog runs out thinking, 'I'm not not to get blamed for this one!' Eventually the landlord kicks him out, but not before the pub has emptied of people and the carpets have rolled up and died.

The Romantic Rambler writes verses of a pastoral nature, and sends them off to magazines such as 'England's Own'; there they are printed in a twee section called 'Rhymer's Corner'. They all go something like this:

> *Oh pensive Arseolethorpe, loveliest of the dale*
> *By thy streams I've wandered in sunshine and in hail*
> *Thy lovely maids I've seen at cottage door*
> *When I've come down from wandering on the moors.*
> *Black are the marble cliffs which beetle o'er*
> *Thy friendly slate roofs and thy chimneys smoking sure.*

It goes on like this for hundreds of lines and is about as interesting as a night out at the launderette.

The Strumpet Rambler

The Strumpet Rambler wears skin-tight tee-shirts, skin-tight shorts and skin-tight skin. Her woollen socks are kept up with black lace suspenders which she wears under her shorts, her perfume repels every mosquito and gnat within a radius of ten miles and her rucksack converts into a mattress at the pull of a special thong. That's all I know about the Strumpet Rambler, because I've never met one myself – but our vicar has. Apparently he told her she was on the path to perdition.

'Bugger me!' she cried. 'Lost again. I thought this path went to Nooky Bottoms!'

The Feminist Rambler

The Feminist Rambler refuses to be helped over stiles, puts her own tent up, and kills bulls with her bare hands. Most of them are very pleasant people and tend to treat men as semi-human beings. The ones I can't stand are the strident Feminists who want to send all men to desert islands and have their children by artificial insemination or whatever they call it. If they hate men so much, why do they expend so much effort trying to look like them?

Marxist Ramblers

Marxist Ramblers tend to have no sense of humour and to interpret everything in the light of dialectical materialism. Discussions on the role of the proletariat in the evolution of the sandwich during the Industrial Revolution can be a bit trying when you're attempting to put a tent up and cook a meal while under constant attack from twenty million Scots midges on the shores of Loch Ness. Anyway, Marx never walked anywhere in his life – he borrowed Engel's bike.

Right-Wing Ramblers

Like Military Intelligence and Young Conservative, Right-Wing Rambler is a contradiction in terms. Rambling implies a sense of freedom, of liberation, and a belief in the right of all people to enjoy the wide open spaces of the land. It also implies a degree of sensitivity and a certain degree of caring about the countryside.

The Right-Wing element within our country think of the countryside in terms of shooting and killing things, as quickly as possible, and clearing off to Mustique afterwards. If they could get away with it, they would build a cable car up Hevellyn and open a big McDonalds hamburger joint at the top. They are to the countryside what Herod is to child-minding.

How to be a Rambler

If you don't want to qualify for any of the above categories from Death or Glory Rambler to Strumpet Rambler, then I suppose you'll want to come under the description of Bog Standard Rambler.

It's dead easy to become a Bog Standard Rambler, all you need is a pair of legs or something resembling them, something to stop them wearing out at the ends (*i.e.*, boots or shoes); some clothes to stop you getting cold and some others to stop you getting wet, something to eat and drink and something to carry it in.

On your Rambles you will have to avoid falling off things, down things or in things. You will also have to avoid getting lost. This is best done by not rambling any further than your front garden but can also be achieved by learning to use a map and compass. This is easy, and if you follow the Marie Celeste Patent Compass Reading Method, you'll be able to ramble all over from John O' Groats to Land's End.

A compass needle always points North; so if you want to go to John O' Groats, you walk in the direction the needle is pointing. If you want to go to Land's End, you walk in the opposite direction. If you want to walk anywhere else other than to John O' Groats or Land's End then it all gets a bit more complicated.

You see there are three Norths – not just one. There's Magnetic North, True North and Grid North. Magnetic North is where the needle of the compass points. Grid North is the direction in which the lines on the map run, and True North is where North would really be if it would stop faffing about.

As if that wasn't complicated enough, Magnetic North doesn't just stay where it is but changes from year to year, so that when you're reading a map you have to allow for magnetic variation. It's only a few degrees, but a few degrees on a ten-mile walk can mean you walking off a cliff or under a train. All in all, compasses can be dangerous things and you're better off using a ball of string.

To navigate with a ball of string using the Hansel and Gretel Navigation Method, you post the string to where you want to go, the summit of Scafell Pike, for instance (not forgetting the post code, of course) keeping hold of the other end of the string. All you have to do then is follow the string from your house to the top of Scafell, not forgetting to wind it up as you go along. We don't want the countryside littered with bits of string, do we?

Map reading is incredibly easy and can be learnt in a couple of centuries by anybody with a first-class degree in Geography or doctorate in Mathematics.

When you look at a map you are looking at a three-dimensional landscape translated into two-dimensional terms, which means that somebody has pinched a dimension somewhere. It's all very well for the Ordnance Survey to tell you not to worry, but that missing dimension is the dimension of up and down and is probably the most important of all since knowing where you are in the third dimension can mean all the difference between being all right and bits of you being found hanging from trees or stuffed down rabbit holes *etc., etc.*; *i.e.*, you would be a bit dead.

The Ordnance Survey have tried to get over this problem of the missing third dimension by using contour lines. Contour lines were unknown to the earliest map makers, who just drew little mountains and wrote 'Beyond Here Be Dragons' whenever they came to a dangerous bit. The problem of how to show a mountain on a flat piece of paper was solved by a man called Jim who worked at the Ordnance Survey. 'Your job,' they told him one day, 'is to work out how to draw mountains on the maps.'

Well, Jim went home and worried about this for some time. He came up with a few ideas that were later abandoned: first they tried making the maps three-dimensional, so that you walked round the countryside with a whacking big papier mache model of wherever it was you were walking. A few people tested this, but the maps went soggy in the rain and the Ramblers were blown away in the wind, as they were holding them.

One night Jim was just about to lift the razor blade to his jugular when his wife came in from Weight Watchers and, stripping off down to bra and pants, lay down on the hearth rug in front of the fire and started to do her exercises . Her circle-stitched bra pointing at the ceiling,

illuminated by the flickering firelight, gave Jim an idea; and after he'd carried it out he put his clothes back on and thought about the mountains again. In a flash it came to him! The circle-stitching on the bra formed lines around the fabric covering his wife's bosoms in a way that could be translated into cartography. The next day Jim set off for the hills, with hundreds of men carrying balls of string. He got them to run round the hill with the string at fifty-foot intervals then, going up in a balloon, he drew what he saw – a method of cartographic surveillance that is used to this very day.

So there you have it: all you need to become a Rambler. You need:

(a) to know what sort of Rambler you want to be
(b) some clothes and shoes to wear
(c) something to eat
(d) somewhere to go
(e) something to help you find your way about (*e.g.* map, compass, ball of string, policeman, Girl Guide or Brownie).

And may the Lord have mercy on your soul.

Chapter Two

The World History of Rambling from Caveman to Astronaut
– Great Historical Rambles and Ramblers from the Wandering
Jew to Genghis Khan, from Baden Powell to Mao Tse Tung and
the Bloke Next Door's Dog

History does not tell us at what stage Man first began to Ramble. Ancient cave paintings at Lascaux suggest that it was when Man first discovered that he stood a better change against the sabre-toothed tiger if he stood up on two legs and moved about a bit instead of wobbling around on all fours.

Other sources point to the invention of shoes and the discovery that they didn't fit too well on the hands as the main reason for people getting off their hunkers and walking upright, but the most interesting explanation comes from professor J.P. Shmecklefumbler at the University of Tel Aviv.

Working through ancient Hebrew and Sanskrit texts he came across a reference to a group of people called the 'Brownnosers', a wandering nomadic tribe who first appeared in the vicinity of the Olduvai Gorge in Africa around the fiftieth millennium BC. Fossil remains discovered in the car park of Fortnum and Mason, Wigan, would seem to confirm the existence of this proto-hominid group and place *Homo brownnosus* somewhere between Neanderthal man and your average football hooligan or South African politician.

An incredible piece of reconstruction work by Dr Hans Orff at Munich University, based on skull size, jaw structure and school photographs, gives us a picture of the

Brownnosers as a hunter-gatherer group of people who travelled on all fours, naked and hairy, across the wastelands of pre-history in single file. The leader (always known as Pinknose), whose position was much envied, would call a sudden halt from time to time – causing a phenomenon known to pre-historians and garage mechanics as 'shunting', and thus earning the Brownnosers their name.

Primitive man soon learned that it was far preferable to travel upright whenever possible, and the Brownnoser people of the Dawn of Time disappeared into the mists of history (visibility down to two millennia) although rumour has it that descendants of the Brownnoser people are still to be found in politics, in most major business organizations and throughout the broadcasting industry.

Although there is still a lot of controversy concerning the earliest evidence of Rambling, most historians agree that Rambling, as we know it, began somewhere in Mesopotamia around 4000 BC. The Epic of Gilgamesh describes how Gilgamesh, fed up with working in the wax-tablet factory where he was a quality controller picking the fluff, dead flies and bits of toenail out of the hot wax, left work one afternoon never to return.

It was assumed that he had been eaten by a crocodile or had fallen down a pit of snakes, both of which were the usual fates of those who didn't turn up for work in those days. On the contrary, however, Gilgamesh had been to the Hammurabi Army and Trireme stores and bought himself a pair of ex-Army sandals, a water canteen and a map of the desert. This was basically a piece of brown wax tablet with a dot in the middle and words beside the dot which read, 'If you are here then you are lost'. Undeterred, Gilgamesh set off into the desert singing, 'I Love To Go A-wandering Along the Mountain Track'. He was eaten by a tone-deaf lion and lives now only in legend.

It has for long been argued that Zeus, the greatest of all the Gods in Greek mythology, was one of the boss Ramblers of all time. Opinion differs as to his importance and a lot of experts disallow his claim to the title on the basis that he travelled round much of the time disguised as a swan, although his mother has pointed out that he wasn't that kind of boy. However, legends concerning a swan with hiking boots walking through Olympia shouting, 'Take me to your Leda', do abound in the islands of the Aegean Sea, although this has been put down to the influence of too much ambrosia.

Narcissus was another Rambler of Greek mythology. He came to a sticky end when he knelt down to get a drink of water from a stream and turned into a flower; which just goes to show that you should always take your water purifying tablets with you wherever you go.

Beowulf was a great Rambler of Norse mythology, although he had a lot of trouble at the Heorot Youth Hostel when one of the hostellers, a well-known tearaway and monster called Grendel, got a bit out of hand and started tearing his fellow dormantarians limb from limb. This was not unusual in the Norse youth hostels of the time but when Grendel started eating a couple of the Ramblers it was generally considered that he was out of order. Beowulf shouted 'Time!', and hacked off Grendel's head and arm – nailing them above the hostel door as a warning to other would-be troublemakers.

Some tell-tale went and snitched what had happened to Grendel's mother. She was understandably upset about the good hiding old Beowulf had handed out to her Number One Progeny – after all, it's not every day one of your family is dismembered and used as a doorknocker. She got her mad up, and came round to Beowulf's house, determined to give him a good belting for what he'd done to her favourite monster son. Though Beowulf was a Norse Boy-Scout type and he didn't believe in killing

women he didn't know on a Friday, he thought it was a bit out of order when she tried to drown him in the lake; so he took out his sword and made a pork jig-saw of her, too. Half-time score: Beowulf 2, Family Grendel 0.

However, Beowulf was not destined to swing his sword round much longer. After a night out on the ale with the lads, celebrating the good job he had done on clearing the footpath of monsters, he set off next day to collect his Duke of Edinburgh award, or whatever the Norse equivalent was in those days. On he went, whistling 'I Love to go A-wandering' in Old Norse, minding his own business and feeling pretty pleased with himself. Sixty miles and two monsters in three days with new boots, and nothing to show for it but a couple of blisters is good going by anybody's standards, when suddenly, and without any prior warning, he was attacked by a non-dairy dragon on a public footpath. Though he fought bravely, and the dragon was in contravention of several by-laws, and the Geneva Convention ('Dragons to eat maidens only during the season, warriors and Ramblers only when there is an 'R' in the month' – it being May, the dragon was definitely in the wrong), Beowulf obeyed the country code and, refusing to use his axe on a public footpath, was torched by the dragon until he was severely dead. He was buried at sea, the worst fate that can befall a Rambler.

Don Quixote de La Mancha has long been seen as the patron saint of Ramblers and together with Baron Munchausen ranks high in the pantheon of Rambler gods. Quixote is a fake, however, and is known to have used a clapped-out rag and bone man's pony for much of his rambling which contravenes code 657B in the Rambler's Rule Book:

Ramblers shall not use ponies or donkeys for anything other than stepping stones, sunshades or filling for pies.

It is obvious that Quixote, who travelled almost everywhere on a mobile, hay-powered glue factory, is disqualified from any claim at all to the title 'Rambler'.

However, it is philosophically that Quixote can be considered a Rambler. There is something endearingly Rambler-like in his bemused optimism, and his ability to get himself into trouble and out of it without even realizing he's been in it. Who but a Rambler, for example, would attack a windmill thinking it was a giant or would mistake a brothel for a youth hostel?

Baron Munchausen, another famous character in European fiction, could, with some confidence, be said to be the father of Ramblers since he travelled aimlessly in every direction, and usually lied famously about the places he had visited, making most of them up and inventing fabulous creatures to inhabit them. This doesn't seem to be a phenomenon that has died out, and I believe sincerely there's a fair chance that places like Billericay and Ecclefechan do not in fact exist. They are deliberate and fantastic creations or figments of some Rambler's fevered imagination; I know lots of people who claim to know people who've been to both places but, like the Yeti of the fabulous land of Shangri La, for me they only exist in hearsay.

The photographs they've shown me of both Billericay and Ecclefechan have been so blurred and indistinct that they could in fact be photographs of creases in a blanket taken on a grey day in a darkened room or a picture of an unwashed navel taken with a greasy lens. Like the flying saucer and the politician's promise, the tales that Ramblers tell must be looked upon simply as folk myths with no real basis in the world as we know it.

Diogenes, another character from mythology, who had the misfortune to be married to Stergene (the goddess of sink tops and soft woollens) has often been cited as an example of a great Rambler since he spent his entire life walking the wide world through. Diogenes, however, can hardly be counted as a rambler at all since he travelled the world with a great purpose: carrying a lighted lamp before him, he went on his way searching all over the earth to find an honest man. I don't know what he was going to do when he found him, unless he was going to play cards with him. Perhaps 'Dodgy Knees', as he was known to the lads, was fed up of people cheating him at pinochle and chase-your-aunt. I know that if he'd gone in the pub I go in and played dominoes there with the locals, they would have rooked him of so much money that he would have smashed his lamp and gone back to living in a barrel or wherever it was he came from.

One of the most unsuccessful Ramblers in history was, of course, Ulysses who was greatly troubled with pigs and sirens and one-eyed giants on the footpaths. The book that was written about him by James Joyce is one of the worst biographies ever written since it never mentions Ulysses in its 643 pages but goes on and on at great length about a Jewish gentleman called Mr Bloom whose wife is being unfaithful to him with a fireman called Blazes Boylan in Dublin in 1906. The book mentions Buck Mulligan, who I think is a cowboy, some cockle pickers and a man called Stephen Dedalus. It also has a bit in it about some burning kidneys and a cat and a very erotic bit at the end, but as my gran said, 'Divil the word about the Cyclops or them pigs of Circes'. I suppose I'm not the first one to point it out but if you want to read a story about a Greek matelot who pokes out a giant's one good eye with a burning telegraph pole, you won't find it here.

It is only when we get to biblical times that we come to the real heroes of Rambling, such as the Wandering Jew. For some reason, the poor gentleman went away from the Crucifixion on Calvary, doomed to wander the earth until the second coming or the End of Time, whichever came first. He was seen recently wandering along the Pennine Way near Mankinholes, his two-thousand-year-old cagoule in rags and tatters, singing rude songs in Aramiac. Rumour has it that he complains continuously that his children never come to see him – but is this surprising if he never leaves a forwarding address?

Moses was the founder of the world's first Kosher Rambling Club and it is to him that we owe the first maps of the Red Sea area. Moses was lucky in having the maps with him on the day that Pharaoh's gamekeepers were legging it across the desert after him, since he was the only one who knew where the stepping stones were. Moses, it is known, had a great deal of trouble with his walking stick – it kept turning into a snake, causing him to fall over in the sand, much to the amusement of all the other Kosher Ramblers who (like all Ramblers) couldn't bear a smart-arse. He was also rumoured to be the most constipated Rambler in history since, as it says in the Bible, 'He took two tablets and went into the mountain and was there for forty days.' It also says later in the Bible that 'the lot fell upon Ahab' but this is thought to refer to something else entirely. Modern biblical scholars believe that what Moses came down from the mountains with was the first Country Code and the ability to light fires in bushes in wet weather.

When Pharaoh tried to block the public footpath that would have allowed the Chosen People Happy Wanderer

Rambling Club, as they called themselves, to leave the House of Bondage Bunk House Barn where they had not been very happy (at least most of them weren't), Moses (Big Moshe to the lads) visited various plagues on Pharaoh and the land of Egypt such as plagues of boils, frogs and junk-food restaurants. It wasn't until Big Moshe called down the plagues of accountants and double-glazing salesmen, however, that Pharaoh finally gave in and moved the pyramid off the footpath, leaving the Chosen People Rambling Club free to get on with their walk and arrive at the tea-rooms in time for last orders – milk and honey and bagels and lox all round.

Julius Caesar was quite a Rambler until he backed into a tent peg on the streets of Rome; he had led several Rambles all over Europe and North Africa in his time. It was in North Africa that he formed the Upper Nile Rambling Club leaving Mark Antony behind as treasurer and Cleopatra as walks organizer. Mark Antony ate something that didn't agree with him, like a dagger or something, while Cleopatra was bitten by her bra and died, a sad fate to befall to fine Ramblers.

Caesar's Rambles brought him on two occasions to the shores of Britain; legend has it that the first time they arrived at Calais, the rest of the lads in the Colosseum Ramblers refused to cross the Channel in the belief that if they did, they'd fall off the end of the world.

They weren't far wrong. When they reached the south coast of England and saw the rows and rows of mud bungalows lining the seashore and the millions of old age pensioners with hearing horns and stone teeth who were the retirees of the Costa Geriatricus, as Caesar called that area (now known as Bexhill-on-Sea and Eastbourne), it did indeed look like the end of the world. Things didn't get much better for the Colosseum Ramblers once they got

inland, for they immediately found themselves set upon by woad-covered farmers, like Caractacus and Cunobelinus, who accused them of trespassing and shot at them with twelve-bore spears and arrows. On their way towards what is now known as Colchester they fell foul of Druids on the footpaths and after a noisy fracas ended up with severe mistletoe rash and hemlock blisters.

Caesar's *Commentaries* are full of reports of harassment and rudeness that make a present-day raging bull on a footpath seem a mere bagatelle. The high spot of Caesar's first trip was an altercation on a bridleway with a woman charioteer who had fitted scythe blades to the wheels of her off-road, four-wheel-drive, two-horse-power Suzuki. She later claimed in St Albans magistrate court that she used the cart to keep down the thistles in her belladonna patch, but she was fined forty axe-heads and ordered to pay compensation to the twenty-four Ramblers who had had to have wheels fitted below the knee.

Hadrian, Caesar's successor as leader of the Colosseum Ramblers, fared a little better, although when he reached the borders of Scotland he did fall foul of the arcane

Scottish law of trespass: a law that few people understand to this day. Basically, it states that nobody is guilty of trespassing until they *are* guilty of trespassing; at which time the landowner or aggrieved is entitled to personally kill them with whatever means is at his disposal, except malt whisky or his teeth.

What caused the Romans most problem in their relationships with the Hibernian Celts, however, was not trespass or human sacrifices on footpaths, but the bagpipes. In those days the bagpipes were not the fine musical instruments they are now with their humming drones and swirling chanter and their stirring tone that can inspire men to leap out of trenches to face overwhelming odds or cry at international matches when 'Amazing Grace' or 'The Flower o' the Forest' echoes round the stadium. In Hadrian's day the bagpipes sounded like several cats breaking wind while one of their number was being encouraged to sing by somebody squeezing its nuts with a tailcracker.

In fact, this very closely approximated to what was happening. The bagpipes were invented by a hairy Celt (referred to in Hadrian's memoirs as Bilious Connelius), an alternative Druid and musician, who discovered that if you took forty cats and put them in a plaid bag with the tails of several of them sticking out, you could, if you placed the bag under your arm, bite the tail of one of the cats while you twisted the tails of the others. The resulting noise was used at dances and weddings to cover the noise of the fighting and generally to make people feel merry and gay – which probably explains why people in Scotland drink so much.

So aghast were the Romans at the noises reaching their campsite from the Border hills that they built a huge wall from Solway Firth to the mouth of the Tyne to keep out the hairy Celts and their bags of cats. Later on, a series of youth hostels were built along the wall at Housesteads, Twice Brewed, Wallsend, Carlisle and other such beauty spots. The wall fell into disuse when somebody invented ladders and the Romans, fed up with the northern winters getting under their togas, went back to Italy. It wasn't long before hordes of Celts in forty-seater chariots, with St Andrew's cross painted on them, were roaring off down Watling Street in search of mayhem and disorder, and hitting cows with the empty McEwans Export cans they threw out of the window.

One of the most famous Ramblers of all time was, of course, Hannibal – who was a Carthaginian, although his mother said he wasn't that sort of boy. He formed the Jumbo Rambling Club and set off on a tour of the Alps, heading for Rome with several thousand club members and a sort of mobile canteen in the form of 'big mobs' of elephants as they say in Australia. The elephants were supposed to be for the Ramblers to kill along the way for

packed lunches, the re-soling of boots, ivory toothpicks, dominoes, *etc.*, but the lads got so attached to them that they burst out crying at the very first tea-time and refused to kill them. The elephants followed them round on their Rambles all over the Alps, followed closely behind by thousands of people with brushes and shovels – collecting the fallout for the roses.

After the Romans came the Visigoth and Vandals Mass Trespass Team, who were so ardent in their pursuit of the looting and raping aspects of Rambling, that they got very drunk on some cheap wine they bought from somebody who said it had fallen off a chariot ('Nudge, nudge, say no more. Know what I mean John?'), and kicked down the gates of Rome. This resulted in the famous 'Rucksacking of Rome', as a result of which a lot of Visigoths had their YHA membership cards taken from them and ceremoniously ripped up there and then, on the spot while they stood there, without further ado.

While the vibram soles of the Visigoths were trampling through the vineyards of Tuscany, the fledgeling Hiking Viking Ramblers Club were setting out from the shores of their native Norway and Denmark. At first they made simple day Rambles, and later on, much longer trips. Then their dragon-headed boats could often be seen moored outside Lindisfarne Youth Hostel, but their habit of lighting the morning fire with a couple of monks got them into trouble with the warden, and he put them on greasy plate and sooty stove duties for a week.

Not content with causing a lot of bother amongst the poor Geordies of Jarrow and Cullercoats, the Viking Ramblers moved further inland on subsequent visits until they reached as far as the Isle of Man and Dublin. There they became so deranged by all the Guinness they drank

that they returned home from the Manx trip convinced that the people there had three legs – a legend which has persisted to this day. It arose when two Vikings, on their way home from the Jolly Tinwald with a belly full of looted Guinness, came across a Manx Rambler helping his mate off with his boot. One man stood up, pulling off the right boot of his pal who, supine on the ground, was invisible to the Danes. They went away shaking their heads and vowing never to drink Guinness again – and *never* to play the Isle of Man at football.

In Eastern Europe at this time, things had not been quiet on the Rambling front and Attila the Hun and Genghis Khan had both made their contributions to the world of long-distance walking. Genghis's contribution was the yakskin *yert*, the first bell tent of its kind and a great improvement on the portable mud huts which had been the only things available up to then. Attila's contribution was more debatable, however, and consisted largely of the introduction of freeze-dried enemies' heads into the Hun Rambler's diet.

It was about this time that the more militaristic aspects of Rambling began to be overtaken by the purely hedonistic, and the pleasure-seeking principle became all. Voyeurism being to the forefront of these pleasures it wasn't long before the age of the great Traveller Rambler dawned and names such as Marco Polo (the explorer with the long woolly neck) and Christopher Columbus became household words. A Marco Polo became the name used for a dustbin lid that no longer fits, while an old underskirt, used as a floorcloth, became known as a Christopher Columbus and you can't get more household than that.

Marco Polo is credited as the man who discovered China, which is a bit silly because the Chinese knew it was there all the time, while Christopher Columbus discovered America – for which no one in his street has ever forgiven him. If it hadn't been for Columbus there would have been no Coca Cola, no 'Dallas', no 'Dynasty', no bubble gum, no television quiz games, no Kentucky Fried Chicken and no American Football. It is the general opinion round our way that somebody should have shot Columbus.

The later Middle Ages saw a great explosion in the number of Ramblers who could be seen roaming about at large in the countryside. The highways and byways, the footpaths and bridleways were chockablock with all manner of Ramblers. True, most of them were brigands, cutpurses, coiners, mad monks, forgers, sheep stealers, crazed nuns, pickpockets, beggars, lepers, double glazing salesmen and general ne'er-do-wells but, then again, Rambling always has attracted some of the more extreme fringe elements of our society.

The medieval period saw the advent of long-distance walking, which became so popular it turned into a craze (akin to the hula hoop and Rubik cube of our own time).

Whereas the Rambler of today is content to go rambling in the Forest of Dean or the Quantocks, or is quite happy with a fortnight on Skye, the Rambler of the Middle Ages would stuff a leather satchel with a side of beef, a few hogsheads of sack, a dozen capon and a couple of dozen loaves and set off for Jerusalem or Rome. If he had only a few days off work, he might go only as far as Walsingham or Canterbury. This form of walking was known as a pilgrimage; and very popular it was too – particularly since the tea shops at the end of the ramble didn't just sell the usual 'mug and a wad', but also did a great line in indulgences.

Indulgences are very difficult to get now (in fact, most of them have been turned into lamp bases or plant holders) but if you can get hold of one then it will come in very handy. It is a specially designed voucher aimed at getting you some remission off your time in Purgatory. As everybody knows, this is the place you go to if you manage to avoid getting sent down to Hell but don't quite make it into Heaven. It's a sort of heavenly Borstal, with time off for good behaviour and the great thing about the Middle Ages was that you could buy time off your stretch in Purgatory by going on a pilgrimage, or by paying a few quid in the shrine when you got there and buying an indulgence or two. ('Buy two — they breed in the dark' was a popular myth put about by unscrupulous indulgence sellers in the Middle Ages.) I actually think that indulgences are a good idea and would like to see them reintroduced so that tourist information centres and tea-rooms and such didn't just sell tea and cake and maps and postcards and leaflets describing nature walks round the area but sold indulgences as well. It would be marvellous because, let's face it, most of us who aren't murderers or politicians know that we probably won't go to Hell but we also know that the odds are heavily against us going straight to Heaven as well.

Most of us, in fact, are in for a bit of bird in Purgatory whether we like it or not. How wonderful it would be if we could all buy indulgences, and get a few hundred years off our stretch in the slammer every time we did it!

'Can I have two five-hundred-year indulgences, please? Them nice ones in the window with a picture of Wuthering Heights on them. It's all right, Fred, I'll get these – you got the bacon butties.'

Shrines also sold relics and if you were lucky and all of him hadn't been snapped up in the July Sale, you might get a bit of a dried saint. Locals and people in the know used to get the best bits by sleeping out all night until the sale started. You might get one of his toenails or an earlobe, or at the very least one of his eyelashes, but if you were really unlucky you'd have to settle for a bit of his dog or cat or whatever pet he had. This was really naff and didn't hold much sway in the upwardly mobile stakes. I mean, it's not exactly going to impress your friends at the dinner party if they've all been on a works outing to Jerusalem and got bits of St Mark's arm and St Jude's kneecap and all you've got is one of the legs of St Mungo's stick insect.

Still, Rambling must have been a fairly exciting pastime in the Middle Ages, what with all the indulgences and relics and things. Like everything else, though, it did have its drawbacks. The youth hostels of the time were rife with plague and scrofula, known as the King's Disease – not because he had it, but because the only cure for it was for the afflicted to touch the hem of the king's garment.

I can tell you now that court records show that the king was well pigged off with people grabbing his gear as he was out going walkabout. I can understand it, too. I don't think I'd be right happy if I was out walking with a new suit on, nice new shirt and tie, taking somebody special for a Vindaloo and a bottle of Hirondelle, and half the scrofulous sufferers in town came wobbling up, pawing the clobber. I don't think you'd exactly feel like enjoying yourself after a couple of hundred people with bits of skin falling off them had been rubbing themselves up against you for good luck. No, things were not all sweetness and light in mediaeval times.

One of the most famous of mediaeval Ramblers was a man called Geoffrey Chaucer. He was a member of the Cheapside Ramblers and ran a small off-licence down near

the docks. He was a great favourite at the Rambling Club Christmas dinners, because every year he would make up a poem about the annual club pilgrimage to Canterbury, with stories about the members who went on it and the people they met along the way. These were collected and put into a book called *The Canterbury Tales* (still available from most good bookshops or direct from the author, G. Chaucer, 14 Coney Street, Cheapside LC1A ZP) and very funny some of them are too. Recently a manuscript was discovered wrapped round a bottle of cheap Italian anti-freeze in an off-licence in Chiswick that Middle English experts now believe is one of the missing poems from the *Tales*.

Although excerpts from it have been reprinted in *The Times Literary Supplement* and *The Harvard Review*, it is reproduced below in its entirety for the first time.

THE RAMBLOURS TAYLE BI GEFRY CHAUCER

A Ramblour there was, y cleped Ron
That hadde grette bootes and ruckesacke on,
Withe mappe and compasse did he roame the hilles
Singen and laffen and nevere tooke no illes,
A mightee manne and one who loved goode ale,
Ande as we walked he tolden us this tayle.

There was in Cheepeside once brutheres three
That worken in a codpiece factoree
At weekends would they trampe the countreeside
Ande walken miles and miles. One Whitsuntide
As smalle burdes were y-singen in the trees
And blossoms were y-tremblen on the breeze,
They tooke the intercity oxe carte
Ande roden many miles to northe partes.

'Strippen me pinke, cor blimey,' one did shoute,
'Don't people 'ere talke funny! Leave it oute!'
'Alle this "Bi Gumme" an '"Tripe and cowheels" crappe!
'Why cante they talke like ordinary chapes?'

While rambouling in the hilles theye mette three maydes
Thatte were amungste the grasse ande heather layde
The sun it being hotte these maydes caste oute
Their skirts, their chemises, yea all their cloutes!
'Allo darlins catchin the old currante bunne
'On your bristols and bottles?' lewdely asked one.
'Eee! tha talkes reete funny laddes!' one lasse didde saye
'We cannot understande thee – go away!'

The seconde brothere steppen to the fraye
And withe a looke of lecherie didde saye
'Come onne darlins, leave it oute cor blimey!
'We can sitte an ave a bunneye, cante we?'

Butte the seconde chappe no bettere didde thanne firste
And the lasses lafen till theye were fitte to burste.
'Nay I'll be beggered!' said one comeley lasse
'I've not had such a laughe since Michaelmasse laste
'When Uncle Ernie wente and goosed the cooke!
'Tha talkes like loonies lads – Scramme! Slinge thy ooke!'

The thirde chappe he clevere was thanne the reste
And madde his minde to ende this merry jeste
And oute frome his ruckesacke he tooke
A Berlitz Northe – Southe phrase booke...
'Ay up lasse! Does tha fancy a goe?' he quoth.
'Now tha's talken!' said the lasses. 'Gerrum offe!'

MORAL
If in foreigne climes you rambouling bee,
Always takke a phrasebooke and a diccionarie!

It's sad to see how this poem, written all those hundreds of years ago, still reinforces sexual stereotypes. I'm pleased to see that it has in fact been excluded from the *Feminist Book of Penguin Verse*, together with most of the rest of English bawdy verse. It is strange, too, how although it was written in the Middle Ages the events described in its iambic pentametre rhyming couplets could have happened yesterday, and probably did, and the day before, and most likely tomorrow as well.

After the Middle Ages nothing much of any note happened in the Rambling world until the arrival of the Tudors. It was then that Good Queen Bess, as the king was known at that time, founded the British Empire Rambling Club, an organization which can only be looked upon with shame and regret by all good Ramblers since its members went on Rambles all around the world wrecking youth hostels, looting, pillaging and causing mayhem.

It all began with a Rambler called Walt Raleigh who, on a walking tour of Cadiz, got into a fight with some Spanish Ramblers in a pub called the Merry Misanthrope. This ended up with half the town being blown up, and the King of Spain's beard being set alight. We condemn football fans for wrecking ferries on trips to the Continent but compared to what Raleigh and his pals got up to, the antics of the football hooligans look like a family row, what with wrecking the coaches of the Armada Ramblers and going to America and pinching all the Indians' potatoes.

I never understand why English schoolchildren are taught to admire Raleigh since he was what my Irish grandmother would have described as a 'thundering blaggard of the direst hue' (had she used that sort of language), who ran round looting and murdering and gave the world nothing but smoking and the french fry, or chip as she is known. Funny sort of hero.

Unfortunately, Raleigh set a very bad example and during the days of Empire-building, members of the British Empire Rambling Club, like Clive of India and Cecil Rhodes of Rhodesia, went round the world finding little black men and saying things to them on the lines of 'Hello, there! My name is Cecil Rhodes, but you can call me Boss!' We're still paying for all the damage they caused. (Something has just struck me. It's strange that Rhodesia was so named after Cecil Rhodes, yet they never called India 'Clive'.)

Prior to Rhodes and Clive, there appeared on the scene a very English Rambler who left his stamp on the face of

71

creation, causing mayhem and riot. This was a horrible man, with a boily face, called Oliver Cromwell. In the name of religion, he went round smashing church windows, cutting off king's heads and lighting his camp fires with Irish Catholics. He was another great historical character that my grandmother and other historians have described as a 'thundering blaggard'.

Napoleon Bonaparte was another great Historical Rambler and although he was French, still deserves a mention here. He was right out of the Walter Raleigh school of looting, pillaging 'thundering blaggards'.

Like a lot of dictators, Boney was an insignificant little horror who realized that a good way to make people notice him was to kill them. He also realized that 'image' was very important and very early on in his career sought the aid of an advertising agency. They advised him to wear his hat sideways on and stick his hand inside his jacket as attention-catching devices. They also sent him to speech therapy lessons, which turned his hectoring lisp into tones of smooth reasonableness that only slipped back into sibilant screeching when he was drunk or when his piles were playing him up. Then cries of: 'Thod off you wotten thwines. Thith thaddle ith killing me, and all you do ith laugh!' could be heard all over Lepanto and St Helena. It was, of course, Napoleon who led the first winter traverse of Russia – it was a total flop and it, like so many similar Rambles led by other similar generals, resulted in the deaths of thousands of the men who followed him but not of Boney himself. It has never ceased to amaze me that people who otherwise seem quite normal sensible types are quite prepared, in times of war, to follow the instructions of some Herbert Politician or Wally General and walk off bravely but stupidly to die while the generals and politicians stay bravely and cleverly in the bunker.

I'm a great believer in the 'cock-up and wally' theory of history and, having met quite a few British Army officers in my time, as well as a few politicians, I have reached the conclusion that they've been able to get away with it for so long because nobody has tumbled to the fact that if a common soldier makes a mistake he gets killed, while if politicians or generals make a mistake they kill a lot of people and all they lose is their seat in Parliament or their rank. And while the poor swaddies' bones are mouldering somewhere in the field in France or a jungle in Burma the general and the politician retire to Berkshire to write their memoirs which are then serialized in *The Sunday Times* and make them a fortune.

Napoleon's unsuccessful Rambles in Russia, by the way, led to him being banished to an island called Elbow and losing the leadership of the Gallic Rambling Club while a Russian mouth-organ and spoons player called Tchaikovsky wrote a very rude overture about it based on the odds the bookies were offering on Napoleon ever getting off again.

The Mormon religion was invented by a man called Joe Smith and an angel called Moroni, to give all the young men in America with crew cuts, steel-rimmed glasses and suits, something to do. He sent them all over the world, knocking on people's doors and asking them to join his club. One of the rules of the club was that you could have as many wives as you wanted, but couldn't drink stimulants. This seems a fair trade-off to me, although you'd think you'd need something to keep you going, what with all those wives and that.

One of the early members of the Mormons was a man called Brigham Young. He founded the Mormon Ramblers and took them all on a long walk out into the desert. After rambling round for a bit they discovered that there was nowhere that they could get a glass of non-stimulant for miles, and decided to build their own city in the desert. It took a long time, because all the wives kept arguing about the wallpaper and where the cooker was going to go, but in the end they managed it and called it Salt Lake City (as against Salt Beef City which had been founded by Moses).

It was during the late nineteenth and early twentieth century that the last of our Great Historical Ramblers appeared on the scene. These are (again in no particular order), Adolf Hitler, Baden Powell, Mao Tse Tung, Colonel Leonid and the bloke next door's dog.

Adolf Hitler, as I said previously, was a hiker rather than a Rambler, in that he had a very definite purpose in all

his Rambles but I'm including him in my list of great
Ramblers because he was very good at organizing mass
Rambles.

It's not everybody who can get up at the Nuremberg
Rambling Club dinner and say: 'Right everybody. Listen
carefully! As soon as you've finished your pudding, we're
going to invade Poland! You'll find packed lunches and
maps of the route at the door on the way out. Don't forget
that you'll need waterproofs and a spare jumper.'

Mao Tse Tung went on what is know as Mao's Long
March, a sort of long-distance walk, which resulted in the
formation of China as we know it today. One result is that
you can now get chicken foo yung with fried rice, crispy
noodles and an extra portion of spare ribs until midnight
almost anywhere in the world today.

Baden Powell is the man who invented Boy Scouts, for
which generations of vicars and the *News of the World* have
been eternally grateful. He also wrote a book called
Scouting for Boys which tells you how to light fires by
rubbing two pyromaniacs together, how to live for a week
without food by sucking a pebble (pamphlet now available
from the DHSS) how to track thieves by their spoor and
how you can wear the same set of underwear for a year if
you beat it regularly with a stick. He made a great
contribution to the world of Rambling.

Colonel Leonid was a Russian astronaut who in the
1960s became the first man to walk in space, thereby
beginning a new era in Rambling: 'Today Ilkley Moor,
tomorrow Betelgeuse!'

The bloke next door's dog might not seem to have any
relevance to the world of Rambling to you, but it does to
me because it's always rambling into my garden and
digging up what scrubby bits of flowers we've got. Added
to that, it's always doing big jobs on our front path; only

last week one of the dustbin men slipped in one while he was carrying the bags out to the rubbish cart and put his back out. He threatened to sue me, and when I told him it was next door's dog that had done it, he said that didn't matter and it was the same as apples falling over my side of the fence from next door. I said it wasn't an apple he'd slipped in but a pile of big jobs; he said it was the same thing and that, because it was on my land, it belonged to me. I said that in that case I was going to report him to the police for stealing my property on his boots.

Our lawyers are at present working on the situation.

Chapter Three

Rambling and Art – Painting – Great Painters who Rambled
– Great Painters who Didn't – Poetry – Rambler Poets:
Wordsworth, Coleridge, W.H. Davies, J.P. Drinkpootle,
McGonagall – Rambling and the Worlds of Music and Dance
– Songs of Rambling

The world of Nature has for long been an inspiration to
painters and poets, writers, dancers and musicians and even,
to some extent, lovers (let's face it, some of Casanova's
greatest work was done, so it is said, under haystacks or in
hedge bottoms) but the influence of Rambling and the
landscape on 'Art' as she is taught in school has never been
properly evaluated. Sir Kenneth Clarke did write a book
called *Landscape Into Art*, which explored some of the
aspects of the pastoral, but he ignored Rambling
completely. It is my intention in this chapter to attempt to
remedy this omission, looking closely at the worlds of
music, dance, painting and literature with particular
reference to the influence on pointilism of the spotted dick
they used to serve at Malham youth hostel.

Painting

Landscape first entered into Art through the work of the
apprentices of the later icon painters. The apprentices
were given the job of filling in the backgrounds of the
paintings once the Master had finished painting the Virgin
and Child. It was very boring work because all you were
allowed to paint on what bits of the canvas he'd left you
with was angels, cherubs, fiery dragons and saintly scenes

such as St Jerome knocking the ants out of his thermal vest with a stone or St Catherine inventing the disc brake. The apprentice painters eventually got so fed up with all the boring repetitious work that they started putting bits of sky and hills and rivers and woods into the paintings.

And I can't say that I blame them. I mean, after all, it can't have been much fun for a lot of those apprentice Giottos who'd been up all night grinding their pigments and boiling their linseed oil, to have to stand all day with their varicose veins throbbing, filling in the spaces that the master had left with fat, pink-bottomed babies with wings sprouting out of their shoulder blades. A twelve-hour shift in that Italian heat slapping bits of pink on angel's bums isn't my idea of a good time.

A lot of the 'filler-in painters', as they are known to art historians, were Ramblers and so they started putting in bits of things they'd seen on their Rambles. A bit of a barn near Florence here, and the waterfall that Guiseppe had washed his feet in beside the bed and breakfast in Tuscany there.

It wasn't long before the landscape began to take over and started to dominate the canvas so that the Virgin and Child became smaller. In fact, in some of the later Dutch landscapes by people like Hertz Van Rental, you'd be hard put to find the Virgin and Child at all – they're usually lurking about round the back of a cowhouse or under an apple wagon somewhere.

In England, landscape began to enter into art once painters had realized that you could make a lot more money by painting a rich man and his family outside their Adam mansion, in their Inigo Jones-designed country park, wearing their Coq Sportif doublet and hose and farthingales, than you could by painting bowls of fruit and laughing cavaliers. Let's face it, there's not much you can say about a painting of a bowl of fruit after you've all had a go at counting the grapes. Unless you're related to the artist, you're not going to spend a lot of time discussing whether those tiny squiggles in the corner really are a milkmaid and her swain doing rudies under a haystack, and not just a bit of stray pink pigment that the painter shook off his brush when a wasp crawled up his trouser leg.

Thus began the great age of English Rambling Landscape painting, which saw the finest work of such painters as J.M.W. Turner, John Constable, George Stubbs and Rose Madder. They spawned imitators in their thousands who roamed the mountains and valleys of the British Isles in search of the picturesque, carrying their boxes of Rowney paints, their Lakeland pencils, their easels and their canvases.

They were a determined bunch of artists, these eighteenth- and nineteenth-century painters of the picturesque. As their attempts to depict the landscape in all its glory became more desperate, so their canvases became larger and larger, until one unknown landscape painter from the Isle of Man, who was painting Snaefell on a forty-foot canvas in a gale, invented hang-gliding. Bits of him *etc., etc.*

After that it was very difficult to get landscape painters to work on any canvas bigger than four inches square, and thus was born the age of the English miniature.

The great Turner himself would go out in all weathers to paint the moods of the landscape. On one occasion, during a tour of the Lakes, he asked a passing shepherd to chain him to a rock in a mountain pass so that he could paint a terrible storm that was raging at that time.

'Chain thee oop?' asked the shepherd incredulously. 'Why, tha'll geet all slithert an flayed an bozzert an nithered an storven. Tha knows it's bahn ter plach an bla an girtle an broggin till morn!'

'I'm a great painter and I'm here to paint the rocks,' shouted Turner at the old man as the storm raged around them.

'Thoos a great pillock,' muttered the shepherd. 'Naybody wants them rocks paintin'. They're all reet the colour they is!'

But Turner ignored this old schoolboy joke and insisted, so that in end the old man reluctantly agreed to chain him up, asking for payment for doing so. The fee for chaining somebody to a rock at that time was about fourteen pence, but Turner, who had no sense of the value of money at all, gave him fifty pounds – about ten times the shepherd's annual income.

The shepherd chained the great painter up and went on into Keswick, where he proceeded to drink himself into oblivion, forgetting completely his parting promise to return and unchain Turner when night-time fell.

The storm raged for three days and nights and the shepherd passed happily on into the afterlife, leaving Turner chained to a boulder somewhere under Skiddaw.

And there he would be to this day had not a passing group of Brownies, doing their 'Arctic Explorer and

Home Help' badge, found him and dragged him back to safety.

He was put into bed immediately and stayed there for three weeks, drinking beef tea and gin and seducing the chambermaids, having decided to give up painting and become Mr Potato Head Salesman.

But, unknown to Turner, the painting of the mountain pass had become so besmirched and smudged by the weather and by the handling given it by the Brownies, who carried it none-too-gently back to town, that it had become a confusing swirl of reds, pinks, greys and pale blues. An art dealer from London, who was in Keswick at the time on a peasant-seducing holiday, saw the painting and, giving the landlord of the inn in which Turner was staying a thousand pounds, he waltzed off with it saying it wasn't for him, it was for his niece.

Turner, who had never been paid more than ten pounds for a painting in his life, realized he was on to a good thing and immediately took all the paintings of little cottages with smoke coming out of their chimneys and little urchins with tears running down their cheeks that he'd been working on and smudged them all up, giving them new titles such as 'Mountain Pass in a Storm', 'Thunderclouds Over the Moor With Peasants', 'Steam and Rain' and things like that. Thus was born the age of the Impressionists.

Constable is best known as the painter of such wonderfully idyllic landscapes as 'The Haywain' and 'Flatford Mill' and most critics place him fairly within the mainstream of English landscape painting. What they don't know, however, is that Constable, although he was a Rambler, hated painting landscapes and only did it because he was employed by a firm of jigsaw and chocolate-box-makers. All Constable really wanted to paint was nudes –

great big creamy yellow nudes with big bums and enormous bosoms. On one of the postcards he sent back home to his brother Evenin from a painting trip in Suffolk he wrote:

> Dear Evenin,
> Im fed up with painting trees and water and hay wagons. Wot Id reely like to pent is gurls with big bsms and big bms Sined yr bro John. PS Don't show this card to mm or dd.

Constable did, in fact, paint lots of nudes. All are now in private collections. The sitter for all of them was Roaring Nancy, the daughter of the landlord of the pub Constable stayed in while he was on his painting trips around Ipswich, 'The Chicken's Nose' or 'Parson's Bum', as it was known to the locals.

As though cocking a snook at society, Constable also painted a tiny nude in every landscape. If you look very closely at 'The Haywain' next time you see it on a chocolate box you will just see, in the left-hand corner, a perfect miniature of Roaring Nancy in all her glory.

George Stubbs is included in this chapter because, although he mainly painted horses, he usually painted them in a landscape. He had found that paintings of horses in bedrooms, greenhouses and chip shops did not sell. Neither did paintings of horses playing poker, rowing, drinking beer or eating kippers.

After hundreds of his canvases had been used as plumbers' toolbags, a Rambler who came upon him painting horses morris-dancing pointed out to him that the proper setting for a horse was the open country. His first paintings of horses in the open country were almost as unsuccessful as his paintings of horses enjoying a fondue cook-up; they were paintings of horses swinging from the branches of trees or standing up, leaning against park railings smoking and watching the ducks. He soon got the hang of it, however, and painted pictures of horses in the middle of country parks just standing there doing nothing except being horses. His pictures became very popular and, in thanks to the Rambler who pointed out his earlier mistake, he always painted a couple of tiny Ramblers somewhere in the landscape. If you look between the legs of any of the horses he painted you can usually see a couple of Ramblers wandering in the landscape.

Rose Madder was one of England's few women Pre-Bakelite Painters; she has been sadly neglected by art historians. Born the daughter of a treacle miner in Pendle in 1756, she went on to become a painter at the local ceramic factory where she painted roses on the saucers. Her talents as an artist were spotted by her employer,

Jabez Harbottle, who commissioned her to paint a picture of himself and his family twelve-foot square – he wanted it to hang in his hall beside his Botticelli of 'Venus Drowning' and his 'First Breakfast' by Leonardo Da Vinci. On the day of the unveiling, half the great families of Lancashire turned up at Harbottle Hall to watch Jabez Harbottle pull aside the curtains – and reveal a painting of the Harbottle family skilfully executed on a twelve-foot saucer.

Rose Madder left the employ of the Harbottles shortly after that. She went on to paint thousands of landscapes, only one of which, a painting of a polar bear in the fog in the Lincolnshire fens, has survived.

Meanwhile, on the Continent, things had not been quiet and painters like Van Gogh, Douanier Rousseau and Paul Gauguin were whacking the camel hair on the stretched sailcloth ten to the dozen. Gauguin and Van Gogh were

friends until the Christmas when Van Gogh, who had no money to buy Gauguin a present, sent him his ear in the post. Gauguin, who had ordered a turkey anyway, didn't know what to do with the ear – so he put it on a shelf and forgot about it. In the meantime, Rousseau, not knowing anything of this at all, had sent Van Gogh a pair of earrings for Christmas – but forgot to say on the card who they were from. Van Gogh thought Gauguin was being funny and never spoke to him again. Gauguin thought Van Gogh was funny anyway, and had already decided to go and live on a South Sea island full of naked women so that he wouldn't have to speak to him. Rousseau, who was fed up with them both, went back to the bike-shed he lived in and started smoking funny herbal cigarettes and painting pictures of sad tigers looking out of long grass at black men playing the flute lying down.

Picasso was a great Rambler/painter and was well known around the St Ives area of Cornwall for being a bit of a lad who would dash off a quick oil painting of a lighthouse or a harbour to sell to tourists for the price of a meal and a few beers. After one particularly rough night on the local cider, a kind of scrumpy known locally as 'liverwarp', Picasso woke up and invented Cubsim. When people tried to explain to him that people didn't have square heads and holes in the middle of their bodies he just muttered something that sounded like 'they do now' and carried on splashing the paint on the canvas.

When word of what had happened to Picasso reached Paris, all the painters who'd previously been busy cutting their ears off and painting sunflowers fled to St Ives to drink scrumpy and paint people with heads like Oxo cubes. Some of them drank so much they invented their own school of painting called Surrealism. Their paintings showed soft watches bending over branches, fish wearing raincoats and bowler hats, big brass keys catching fire spontaneously, men with apples for heads and men with bowler hats smoking their noses in their pipes, which just goes to show what happens once Old Man Scrumpy gets a good grip of you.

Poetry

I suppose the best-known nature poet in the English language is William Wordsworth. What is not generally known about him, however, is that all his poems were, in fact, written by his sister Dorothy. The Lake District of Wordworth's day was full of poets. You could hardly walk up the Stake Pass in those days without treading on a poet or two. They were all over the place and were so thick on the ground that the local people were well fed up with 'yon great pillickin poets' as they called Wordsworth

and the thousands of his followers who had flocked to the Lakes.

Like all things, it had seemed a good idea at the time when Southey discovered you could pick up a little cottage in Cumberland for the price of a pie and a pint and a mucky woman in London, and shipped himself off up there. But, being a blabbermouth, he couldn't keep it to himself, and it wasn't long before all the Hampstead loonies were jumping in their Brougham 2CVs and their four-wheel-drive sedan chairs and were hot-footing it up to Westmoreland, buying every tumbledown cottage and pigsty they could get their hands on and sending the price of property sky-high.

What was even worse was that, though they wrote poems about 'the rude peasantry' ('rude' meaning rough and dependable, stalwart and good, in those days), they really couldn't stand them. Apart from seducing one or two of them, and getting a few of them to do the garden or mind Tabitha and Jason while they went to creative writing classes, they had nothing to do with them. This was because the 'blushing maids and venerable Hodges' all around them spoke funny, had pig muck on their boots and didn't swoon at the sight of 'a pensive shimmering eve' or a daisy 'trod careless by a rustic swain'. It's funny that Wordsworth, who spent much of his life trying to write like one of the working class, didn't realize that all about him in the hills were the poems and balladry of the peasantry in their folk songs and their stories. He went waltzing round the Lakes with his nose in the air writing doggerel, while the average shepherd on the hills probably knew hundreds of folk songs that were twice as good as anything old Willy would ever write.

I often wonder what the country people made of Coleridge, De Quincy, Wordsworth and the rest as they staggered round from house to house smoking dope and shouting out lines of poetry at each other across the back garden wall. I think it's funny, too, how generations of schoolchildren in the English-speaking world, from Auchtermuchty to Mombasa, from Bagshot to Bombay, have been taught to learn by heart the ravings of some drug-crazed Hampstead barmpots who would be exposed by the *News of the World* and locked up today.

You can imagine the headlines:

JUNKIE DROP-OUT POETS
IN BEAUTY SPOT HIDEAWAY
DOPE AND SEX ORGY SCANDAL.

It's no exaggeration to say that half the stuff written by the Lake Poets was written under the influence of opium. Coleridge was particularly partial to a puff of the weed, and wrote some very strange poems about men with albatrosses round their necks and one called 'Kubla Khan' which he never finished.

There he was, apparently, reefer clenched between his lips, banging away at the brass and ebony word processor ten to the dozen:

In Xanadu did Kubla Khan
A stately pleasure dome decree;
Where Alph, the sacred river, ran
Through caverns measureless to man
Down to a sunless sea...

He types out another few dozen lines all about this place called Xanadu, a place he's never been to and knows naff all about. All of a sudden the doorbell rings. He gets up to answer it. It's a man from Porlock selling doorbells. Coleridge tells him he's already got one and comes back to the typewriter.

'Now then,' he says to himself. 'What was I doing? Oh
yes!' he says. 'I remember I was writing. Let's have a look.
What is all this? Where the bloody hell's Xanadu? Who's
written all this crap? Mary! That bloody dog of yours has
been at me typewriter again!'

Wordsworth, although he was not the dope fiend that
De Quincey or Coleridge was, did have a lot of personal
problems. Most of them were to do with him getting a lot
of colds and taking things for them that made his teeth fall
out and gave him boils and meant that he was not quite on
the planet most of the time.

His poetry suffered greatly as a result of this, and
Dorothy spent much of her time correcting it and
rewriting it for him. Thus, as I stated before, much of the
poetry we now attribute to Wordsworth was really

written by his sister. The poem 'Daffodils', for example, is reproduced below, as originally written after Wordsworth and Coleridge had spent an afternoon on the magic mushrooms.

REALLY WEIRD
By
William Wordsworth
Child of the Universe
Om Mani Padme Hum

I wandered stonedly as a clown
Sort of floating over the dales and hills
I was stoned man — really stoned
It was heavy man I mean I really started to freak man
There were all these yellow flowers yeah?
I think they call them dandelions or something
And I felt y'know threatened by them, yeah?
There were just so many of them, man
It was so weird! I started saying my Mantra, yeah?
To like get control you know?
But it was so weird there was this atmosphere, yeah?
And these flowers were shaking their heads at me, yeah?
Really negative — yeah?
Course I knew I was near a ley line because
I could like sense it y'know because there were
Really bad vibes, really negative — yeah
Then I woke up and found out
It had all been a dream, yeah?
But it was weird, really weird!

Dorothy Wordworth, realizing that poems like that don't pay the rent, rewrote it so that it read:

I wandered lonely as a cloud
That floats on high etc.

She put it under Wordsworth's pillow, ripping up the original. It was recovered later from the dustbin by De Quincey, who was going through it for fag ends. When he woke up, four days later, Wordsworth found the manuscript under his pillow and took it downstairs to show Coleridge saying, 'Hey, S.T., dig this really wacky poem, it's so sort of weird, I mean I don't even remember writing this stuff, I must have kind of goofed out and freaked off, you know?'

Coleridge hardly looked up from the joint he was rolling saying, 'You think that's weird, man – dig this. I've found out that while I was stoned I wrote an entire poem called "Mnfrxfrxfrx".'

'Mn frx frx frx?' asked Wordsworth, incredulously.

'I have trouble saying it too,' said Coleridge.

'How does it go?'

Coleridge opened a drawer and took out a pile of paper. 'It's a bit long,' he said and before Wordworth could stop him he'd begun reading it in a loud, husky voice, the pungent aroma from his reefer permeating the room.

MNFRXFRXFRX
By
Samuel Taylor Coleridge, Child of the Universe

It is an ancient road digger
He stoppeth one of three
By thy long grey beard and glittering eye
Now wherefore stopst thou me?

'The lamps were filled
The road was drilled
The nightwatchman he came
And sat down by the Brazier
McGinty was his name.

'As night came o'er the glittering town
The poor nightwatchman nods
And came there thieves and they did steal
The shovels, picks and hods.'

'The rotten sods,' interjected Wordsworth angrily.

'No, that would make it one line too many,' said Coleridge. He carried on with his reading, clearing his throat impressively and waving his hand towards the window.

There came the dawn
And with the morn
Then came the navvies bold
And found the nightwatchman asleep
His brazier dark and cold.

RAMBLING AND ART

'How!' said the foreman
'What is this lads?
I swear by Castor and Pollux,'
And turning to McGinty
He said . . .

'How long does this go on for? Only I've got the ironing to do,' asked Wordsworth nervously.

'It goes on for another three thousand lines, man, it's narrative epic this it's not a bloody sonnet! For God's sake.'

'All right man, stay cool,' said Wordsworth, taking the poker out of Coleridge's hand. 'How does it end?'

'They tie a dead cat round the nightwatchman's neck and make him go all round the place telling people stories about dead sailors, then the last verse goes:

There was a young lady called Annie
Who plaited the hairs . . .

'I've heard that one,' interrupted Wordsworth. 'Southey told it me in the pub the other night.'

'It's not the same one,' said Coleridge angrily.

'Go on then,' muttered Wordsworth, looking anxiously towards the door in case Dorothy should come in.

Coleridge cleared his throat.

There was a young lady called Annie
Who plaited the hairs on her . . .

The door opened and Dorothy came in with an egg custard she had made. Coleridge, seeing her out of the corner of his eye, carried on.

Mnrfrxfrxfrx mnrfrxfrxfrx mnrfrxfrxfrx mnrfrxfrxfrx.

'I'm going to do the ironing,' muttered Wordsworth, sidling towards the door.

W.H. Davies was a poet who spent much of his early life tramping the roads of Britain and America until he was discovered by George Bernard Shaw in his beard one day. He went on to write *The Autobiography of a Supertramp*, a sort of dropout's guide to the Universe which tells you how to make a kind of tea by boiling old newspapers, how to fricassee any squashed hedgehogs you find in the road and how to sleep on a washing line. More importantly perhaps, he tells you how to ask someone for the price of a cup of tea when you really want the money for a bottle of cheap Australian plonk. Have you noticed, by the way, how many of the blokes that stop you on the road asking for a few bob, have Scots accents? I don't think they're Scots at all.

I have been approached by Chinese tramps on the streets of Dieppe who've said to me, 'Hey Jimmy, ye wouldnay have a few wee coppers there for the price of a wee cup o' tea an that would yez pal?'

I'm convinced that this is a kind of international Esperanto that you have to learn when you become a down and out. There's probably a BBC Television course called *Get by in Ergot and Slang* with a two-cassette set of tapes for you to get the accent right.

Although better known as a sort of naïve primitive poet, W.H. Davies wrote many poems about the open road, one of which is in fact called *The Open Road*.

THE OPEN ROAD

Oh the open road oh the open road
She's beckoning to me
She's beckoning my blisters
And she's beckoning my bad knees.
It's away unto the mountains
I will go with gentle Annie
The dark-eyed farmer's daughter
Who plaits the hairs on . . . mnfrx mnfrx mnfrx.

Elphinstone J. Drinkpootle, 'The Flawed Poet', was a Rambler poet from Eccles in Lancashire who, during the course of a very long lifetime stretching from Queen Victoria's day until the late 1970s, wrote well in excess of a hundred thousand sonnets, poems, haikus and epic ballads, none of which ever saw life in print. He was not called the flawed poet for nothing; although he had a fair command of language and could write with some poetic style, he was unable to stop himself from writing 'unpoetic' words in the middle of otherwise commendable verse. He was so badly slammed by the critics for this that he wrote a letter to *The Times* in which he stated that he was so upset by their criticism he had decided to make an attempt upon his life. They wrote a letter back suggesting that they be alllowed to do it for him.

Drinkpootle combined several careers, those of poet, wrestler and skrimshanker, with his lifelong hobby of trespassing. He loved nothing better than a KEEP OUT or a PRIVATE sign.

He was then in his element and would set off bravely across wherever it was he wasn't supposed to be, undeterred by any bulls, tanks or gamekeepers that he might meet upon the way. He wrote many of his best poems in hospital and in fact often signed himself Frankenstein since his body, he claimed, contained about as much metal as the monster's.

Drinkpootle sent an average of ten manuscripts off each day to various publishers, desperately hoping to see one poem in print but all his manuscripts were returned with polite rejection slips.

On one occasion, no less than seventeen postmen, who over the years had sustained double hernias carrying Drinkpootle's returned and rejected poems, picketed the front door of the London publisher Faber and Faber hoping to force them to publish Drinkpootle's poems and save postmen yet unborn from a similar fate. All to no avail.

The poetic works remained unpublished until after his death. Sadly, he died while trespassing on a disputed footpath along the course of the Big Dipper on Blackpool Pleasure Beach and his poems were published by a public subscription. It was raised from all the people who'd been in the funfair that day and who claimed they'd never had so much fun as watching Drinkpootle trying to outrun the Big Dipper cars.

The poem reproduced below is from a cycle of poems called *O Sceptred Isle*, in which the poet celebrates the eternal links that have bound the English to the landscape of their island.

HIGH WIND OFF THE YORKSHIRE COAST
By
Elphinstone J. Drinkpootle
The Flawed Poet

Where sandstone cliffs glower above broken bays
Winds whip waves and dally with small ships
Bringing to the shore the sharp salt spray
And to me the smell of fish and chips
I heard the mermaids singing each to each
As I walked in broken light along the beach.
At the tide line I thought of England and the sea
Then I got that funny twinge again in my knee.
I thought of England and all the English sailor dead
And particularly of a bloke in our street called Fred
Who's dead. He wasn't a sailor, but what does it matter?
He was a window cleaner who fell off his ladder.
Then high winds took the coast and shook the salt sea waves
And sea-birds mewed across the sailors' graves.
Except Fred who's buried in the graveyard of
The Jumbo Methodist Chapel in Middleton Lancs.

William McGonagall, the great Scots poet and author of the *Poetic Gems* was, like Robert Burns, a great Rambler poet; he wrote a tremendous number of verses in the bardic tradition. McGonagall was the son of a Dumfries Bailiwick Weaver who wove the six-hundred-foot-long wicks for the great lighthouses of the time. He wrote rambling verse of great sublety and complexity. One of his poems is reprinted below.

THE ATHOL BRIDGE TEA-ROOMS DISASTER
By
William McGonagall

In the year eighteen hundred and seventy-five
Which will be remembered for a very long time
Thirty-seven ramblers did go
On New Year's Eve
Over Ben Muchty in the frost and snow
Which nipped their fingers and made their noses glow.
The midnight struck and they all did cheer
Shouting 'Hip Hurrah' and 'Happy New Year'

All in the year eighteen hundred and seventy-six
Which will be remembered for quite a bit
At Athol Bridge they did stop
For there was a welcoming tea-shop
And in they did go
Out of the snow and the winds that blow
All in the year eighteen hundred and seventy-six
Which will be remembered for quite a bit.
In they did go to order tea and toasted tea-cakes.

'You're aye welcome this night
But I can nae get the tea urn to light,'
Sadly the tea-shop lady did say.
'Give me a match and I will do it right away,'
Cheerily said wee Jock
Who was a staunch bloke.
He turned on the gas and out it came
And Jock rubbed the sulphur on the sandpaper
But brought forth no flame.
Over and over again he struck a match
But they were all wet, alas and alack!
Out and out the gas it came
But still there was no flame
The gas hissed like an Evil Spirit of the night
As wee Jock up to his knees in dud matches
Tried to get a light.
Then 'A flame a flame!' cried all and one
There was a Whumph and a Boom
And they were blown to kingdom come.
Sky-high they were blown and did come down in pieces
Mother and father, sons and daughters, nephews and nieces
Oh heavens! All those poor people were blown to bits
On the first day of eighteen hundred and seventy-six
Which will be remembered for quite a bit.

Rambling and the Worlds of Music and Dance

The great Nijinsky, while on a Rambling tour in the Yorkshire Dales, amazed the residents of the small market town of Hawes by dancing *L'Après-Midi D'Un Faun* in the town square on market day accompanied by George Bernard Shaw on comb and paper and Sarah Bernhardt on spoons. Rucksack on back and boots a-flying he executed the most intricate steps of this innovative dance, to the total amazement of the farmers and their wives who had come down from the hills to sell their cheese and butter and eggs.

The general opinion amongst the bystanders watching was that either he was on a day out from an asylum, had been stung by a horsefly, had been drinking Theakston's Old Peculier or had caught himself in his zip. The last conclusion eventually won the day and a local hardware merchant was summoned from the back of his store. He pushed himself through the throng of people and with an oil can oiled Nijinsky's fly.

Nijinsky, outraged by this – as he believed – assault on his person, fetched the shopkeeper a flying kick under the chin. The ensuing affray resulted in several arrests being made. Amongst those arrested were Nijinsky, the shopkeeper and a particularly strong cheese that had been upsetting everybody all day.

Dance has always played a very strong part in the world of Rambling. The combination of poise, balance and sheer physical strength that is vital for both has meant that over the years many of the greatest dancers have been Ramblers and vice versa.

Fred Liversedge of the Strangeways Prison Tunnelling and Rambling Club was invited to Covent Garden to dance the lead part in an experimental ballet called

Truckers in Wet Leather, while the great Pavlova was leading a circular Ramble around the edge of Kinder Scout.

Fred Astaire and Ginger Rogers once set out to dance the entire length of the Pennine Way, but retired at Hadrian's Wall with third-degree blisters at the same time as a Rambler called Albert Gherkin was delighting theatregoers of Broadway with a new dance craze called 'The Dungeon Ghyll Shuffle'. Happy days.

When a funeral cortege processes through the black quarter of New Orleans, the jazz band that precedes the coffin and chief mourners plays slow marching tunes for something like four blocks. After four blocks the soul is deemed to have left the body and gone to the great tea-room in the sky and the band rip straight into the hottest jazz you'll every hear. One of the numbers that they always play as they lead the body to the cemetery is 'Didn't He Ramble', a number that illustrates beautifully the connection between music and Rambling. This is always followed by 'Didn't He Blister', 'Didn't He Always Get Us Lost' and 'Didn't He Always Disappear When It Was His Round'.

Armies have always sung on the march, for singing, as Baden Powell said, 'Keeps the spirits up, lends a bounce to the step and shortens the weary mile as we march ever on.' Caesar's men sang 'In Bonum Trireme Venus' and 'Genus Sursum Mater Brown' as they set off along the Appian Way on yet another Ramble into Egypt or Gallicia. Napoleon's chaps all sang 'Nous Allons Donner Les Russians Clog Pie' on the way to Moscow and 'Montez Moi La Route Chez Moi' and 'Boney Est Un Grand Pillock' on the way back.

So Rambling and music, therefore, have long been intertwined – like the woodbine and the ivy, like the rose and the briar and like the coiled-up extension lead for the Flymo that always ends up in knots, no matter what you do.

(Have you ever noticed, by the way, that no matter how carefully you coil things like extension leads and hosepipes they always end up as a heap of spaghetti when you drag them out to use them again. I wonder if there's some sort of poltergeist that lurks in garden sheds and cupboards, whose job it is to tangle up the hosepipes and the extension leads of the world. If you were ever to add up the number of man- (sorry) person-hours that have been lost over the years with sailors untangling ropes, DIY fanatics untangling cables, gardeners untangling hoses and snake charmers having to sort their stock out every morning before they can put lips to pipe, I bet the total would be enough to build Troy a couple of times over.)

Over the years this symbiotic relationship between music and Rambling has produced great classical pieces such as Vivaldi's 'Concerto for Mandoline, Beer Tray and Dubbin Tin' and Beethoven's 'Concerto for Braces, YHA Spoons and Leader's Whistle'.

Chopin wrote no fewer than one hundred and ten études for harmonica, comb and paper and tin whistles, while Mozart wrote the most famous of all classical rambling pieces, 'Eine Kleine Knackered Music'.

Wagner composed three song cycles based round the legends of Hairy Jim and His Battles With the Dwarf Gamekeepers on Kinder Scout. In the song cycle Jim is lured across the peat bogs by a group of Girl Guides who are singing 'Gin gan goolie goolie watcher gin gan goo' on a rock in the mist. Lost, tired and exhausted, almost dead and not feeling very well he wanders through the peat, attacked by cramps and crazed killer sheep. Coming at last to Kinder Downfall he meets the Dwarf Gamekeepers who tell him he's trespassing. In the ensuing battle Hairy Jim sings the famous aria 'I'm Kicking A Dwarf off the Edge of The World' then descends into the Merry Underworld for a quick pint and a cheese barm-cake before closing time.

In this century some of the greatest composers have made their contribution to the world of Rambling. One thinks of Holst's Rucksack Symphony and Vaughan Williams' arrangement of Nick Nack Paddy Wack for string, comb and paper. In more recent years, however, contemporary music seems to have lost touch with the Rambling world: in fact Ramblers have been warned off trying to sing Stockhausen since the tragedy in 1984 when his music so depressed several singers that they threw themselves off Cader Idris.

The world of folk and popular music has produced a wonderfully rich crop of ballads and songs related to the outdoor life, some of which have become the theme songs of various Rambling clubs. These include:

These Boots are Made for Walking — *K Shoes Happy Valley Ramblers*

You'll Never Walk Alone — *Croydon Schizophrenics Happy Wanderers*

Didn't He Ramble — *The Lord Lucan Memorial Ramblers*

RAMBLING AND ART

I'm a Rambler and a Gambler and a Long Way From Home —
Ladbroke's Walking Club.

There are other well-known Rambling songs:
'Rambling Rose' is everybody's favourite and her
boyfriend's going to kill her when he finds out. 'Ramble
Away' tells the story of a young man and a young girl
meeting on a public footpath and begins

> *As I was a-going to Derry Down Fair*
> *I met lovely Nancy a-combing her hair*
> *I tipped her the wink and to me she did say*
> *Are you the young man they call Ramble Away?*

The song then gets a bit rude and the upshot of it all is that
the girl ends up 'dans le Club Pudding', as the French so
delicately put it, which only goes to show that blisters and
compass neck are not the only things you can catch while
out Rambling.

Chapter Four

Rambling and Health – Survival and Rambling – Sex and the Rambler – Drugs and the Rambler – Rock and Roll and the Rambler – Diseases of Rambling from Stile Crotch to Wet Grass Bum-Rot – Enemies of the Rambler, Bulls, Insects and the like

General Health

Rambling is generally a fairly healthy pastime, and one that rarely involves its devotees in anything more hazardous than the occasional chance of a bit of nettle rash or an impacted toe-nail, but there are a number of things

that ought to be said concerning the Rambler and various aspects of health.

Firstly, don't overdo it. A number of people die every year on our hills and mountains because they overdo it.

Don't try and ramble too far. Forty miles in a day is about maximum. A number of people have killed themselves and even got into serious difficulty because they set out to go too far in a day and burnt themselves out. One man attempting the Pennine Way in twenty-four hours suffered exploding kneecaps, while another walking round the coastline of Britain in four days wore his legs down to the hips. You can have too much of a good thing, as the hedgehog said when he fell off the scrubbing-brush – even Rambling.

Don't carry too much: waterproof, map, compass, food and drink are about all you need in ordinary conditions. One Rambler found dead last year had suffered a massive heart attack while trying to climb Helvellyn carrying two suitcases, a stereo, a telescope, a stove, several pounds of food, a huge case of cameras and lenses, a hair dryer and an electric blanket. He made it as far as the end of the car park.

Secondly, don't underdo it. You *can* climb Ben Nevis in a snowstorm in a bikini but bits of you will drop off before you get to the top. At least take a flask of hot soup with you, if nothing else. You can pour it over yourself if things get rough.

Thirdly and lastly, if you have any serious medical conditions that might give rise to problems, you should think seriously about not going Rambling. If you are dead, for example, you should stay at home – there's enough dead people driving cars on a Sunday without you adding to the number. If you suffer from Agoraphobia don't go rambling in East Anglia. If you suffer from Xenophobia don't go rambling up Striding Edge on a Bank Holiday and if you suffer from Fee Fie Phobia don't go climbing any beanstalks.

Survival

The main threats to your continued existence on this planet, as a live Rambler, are lack of heat, too much heat; lack of food, too much food; sharp things, blunt things, animals, too much water, no water; big rocks, other people, birds, low-flying aircraft, things falling on you, you falling on things, getting lost, getting found by the wrong people, the earth swallowing you up, the sky falling on your head, goblins kidnapping you.

In fact, with all these threats around it's a wonder anybody goes out at all. Space doesn't permit me to deal at any length with all the threats mentioned above but some hints on survival that may come in useful are listed below.

Cold

Wrap yourself in several layers of bacon fat and wear this under your underwear. This should keep you warm in all but the most severe conditions. But do remember not to stand too close to the pub fire when you come in from the cold. If you forget you could be in serious trouble. At the very least you'll cause a stampede to the bar with people being killed in the rush to order bacon butties. At the worst you could end up well-barbecued and basted, ten stone six of pork scratchings on the hearth rug.

Other ways of dealing with cold are: setting fire to your clothes, getting several people to lie on top of you and keep you warm with their bodies, and getting an animal, *e.g.* a sheep, to lie beside you and keep you warm. (Try explaining any of these away to the police or a

jealous husband/wife/boyfriend/lover, shepherd by the way.)

Heat

Take all your clothes off and lie down. If somebody close by you collapses with the heat, loosen his/her clothes and in extreme conditions of heat exhaustion remove all clothing. While lying there, rehearse excuses you will make to police/husbands/lovers/shepherds *etc.*

Water

Too much water — swim or drown. If somebody else is drowning demonstrate how to swim from the safety of the bank. Remember that when you're drowning your past life goes before you so you'll finally be able to discover where you put that set of keys in 1956 and what that bloke

was called who brought your sister home in 1963 and sold you your first car, that Ford Popular – there it is! It *was* green! I could have won that fiver off our Tommy! Grey he said it was. Stupid berk! There's that girl I met at the tennis club dance. Jane she was called or was it Anne? Just a minute, what's happening here? Ey! I'd forgotten this bit. I remember that sofa and those cushions. Good God, look at that! Doesn't it look funny from this angle? I wasn't half as fat then as I am now. Hang on a minute I'm going to tread water and slow this bit down ... *etc, etc.*
Too little water — Baden Powell states, quite seriously, in the book *Scouting For Boys*, that when you're thirsty you can suck a pebble and that will keep you going for quite some time. Well, pebbles must have been a lot juicier in BP's day because when I tried it all I got was a mouthful of grit and my tongue started wearing out.

If you're thirsty there's only one thing to do. Get a drink – tea, beer, lemonade, water, any of these will do but if you are in what the American Services Survival Manual calls 'a desert situation' and there's nowhere to buy any of these things then you'll probably die.

Sharp things and blunt things
Bulls' horns and barbed wire come under the former category, farmers' comments and landlord's wit come under the latter. Bulls are dealt with in the section on Rambler's enemies. Barbed wire, which was invented by a nun, by the way, can be rendered harmless by several layers of sacking or a stile. You should always have these handy.

Depending on whether you want a belt in the mouth or not you could try any one of the following ripostes to farmers' comments and landlords' wit:

I was like that when I had my first drink too.
If you had brains you'd be dangerous.
You might call it beer but I think the horse wants shooting.
This is a footpath whether you like it or not.
Don't be stupid – it's not loaded.
I'm going but I'll be back with the police!
You can't dump that on a public right of way!
Do you mind! My wife is under there!

Earth swallowing you up, sky falling on your head, goblins kidnapping you

There's not much you can do about any of these things although there is a proprietary brand of goblin repellent on the market, available from most chemists and outdoor pursuit shops, that is said to be very good. (Warning: it does leave funny stains on clothing.)

Getting lost

If you're lost the first thing to remember is don't panic!

Move into a situation where you may more easily be seen by people who may be looking for you, for example, into a forest clearing or on to a skyline. Once there, shout 'Mum' very loudly at one-minute intervals. If she doesn't come, try making the international distress signal. This is three dots followed by three dashes followed by three dots, the Morse code for SOS and internationally recognized

So stand up making yourself as conspicuous as possible and shout very loudly DOT DOT DOT DASH DASH DASH DOT DOT DOT until somebody comes. Don't waste your time by shouting MAYDAY because if it is May people will think you're a Druid, or morris dancer, or some such, celebrating. If it isn't May people will just think you've got the date wrong.

If you're still hopelessly lost, write a letter telling people where you are. Post it in a bottle, if there's a river or an ocean nearby (don't forget the post code). If there's no river close at hand then try and get a passing pigeon to carry it for you or failing that make it into a paper plane and throw it.

If you're lost in the snow you can make the letters SOS in the snow large enough for a spotter plane to see it. How you make it is up to you, but men will probably find it easier than women.

Getting found by the wrong people

If you are very very lost then you may be grateful for anybody finding you. There are certain groups of people it is very unlucky to be found by such as trolls, goblins and boggarts. Repellents for all these can be purchased from stores near you.

Worse still, however, you could be found by cannibals. This is unlikely in Britain since the last cannibal, Sawney

Beane, died over ten years ago but is quite possible elsewhere.

If you are found by cannibals you've a very slim chance of survival, though you could try a few things:

Tell them you're tainted.
Tell them your middle name is Salmonella.
Given that the boiling point of water is 100 degrees centigrade and that at regulo three it takes the average cannibal fire about three quarters of an hour to raise twenty litres of water through fifty degrees centigrade and given that a human being expires at the sixty degree mark, you've got about eighteen and a half minutes to convert them to vegetarianism.

Sex and the Rambler

I don't intend to delve too deeply into this subject since

much of what can be said is self-evident, but there are a few points worth making.

It should only be attempted while stationary.

Don't attempt it anywhere dangerous, e.g. on the edge of a cliff, in a raging torrent or in a crowded tea-room near a boiling hot tea urn.

Don't do it while you're trying to read a map. You'll probably get the compass bearing wrong and could, in fact, shake it off its gimbal.

Don't take any blow-up dolls above 15,000 ft since above this height they are liable to explode. And finally, if you must do it, do it quietly.

For Heaven's sake! People like me come to the countryside for peace and quiet. We don't want to hear all sorts of grunting and puffing and animal and vegetable noises coming from various bushes, clumps of heather and so on, particularly when we're not involved. It's very off-putting.

Drugs and the Rambler

Drugs and drug abuse have crept into many sports now, mainly to their detriment. It would be a shame to see the same thing happen in Rambling. I cannot counsel too severely against the dangers of overdosing on glucose tablets, dubbin sniffing, Mars Bar dependence and liniment addiction. It all begins innocently enough with somebody suggesting that you try it.

'Go on,' they say, 'it's only this once.' But where does that lead us, dear reader? Into the nightmare world of dependence, where the addict craves his or her fix so much that they are prepared to go to any length, even to stealing and selling their bodies, to satisfy their abject cravings. I've seen it in youth hostels and on camp sites throughout the land, people furtively slinking into their sleeping bags well before lights out with a bottle of liniment or a tin of dubbin and in the morning they stand by the fire hollow-eyed and haggard, a parody of a human being.

Rock and Roll and the Rambler

If the rock hits you, you roll — end of story.

Diseases of Rambling

There are a number of diseases, some of them notifiable, associated with Rambling. Rather than go on at any great length about them here, I'll list the most important of the diseases together with any simple remedies or treatments that may be beneficial. If symptoms do persist, however, remember you should always consult your doctor. He may laugh – but can you blame him?

Stile Crotch — found mainly amongst Ramblers of short stature, the symptoms are hard skin on the affected areas,

together with occasional splinters or creosote rash. Difficult to distinguish from Fence Rash but easily distinguishable from Barbed Wire Bum because there are generally no punctures of the skin.

Treatment — built-up shoes can sometimes help, as might the wearing of double seat corduroy breeches. To alleviate the condition once it has occurred, liberal applications of neat's-foot oil over the affected area takes away some of the stinging.

Electric Fence Tear Duct — caused by straddling electric fences in wet breeches. The inflamed tear ducts that occur as a result of this can be very distressing as can the ringing in the ears and the tendency for the sufferer to attract bits of paper and fluff to himself as he's walking along.

Treatment — built-up shoes and portable stiles can prevent the condition returning but the best cure for the complaint, once it has been contracted, is for the patient to either earth himself well with a copper rod or find somebody oppositely charged and rub himself against them. (Try explaining that to boyfriend, husband, lover *etc.*)

Tea Bloat — otherwise known as Peealotsky's Syndrome. Caused by over-indulgence at the thermos. Symptoms: puffiness around the eyes, slurred speech and trembling limbs. In acute cases this complaint can lead to loss of memory and the tendency to see things in black and white and in four dimensions.

Treatment — a diuretic, administered three times a day, can help in mild cases. In acute cases, the patient should eat large quantities of blotting paper or sawdust. In extreme cases, surgery is the only answer and the patient is implanted with a large tap.

Bullphobia and Agoraphobia — symptoms of Bullphobia

are loss of weight, gibbering, slavering, uncontrollable trembling at the sight of meat and the tendency to jump into shop doorways at the sight of anything big and brown. As yet there is no known cure.

Agoraphobic Ramblers have found some relief in recent years since the invention by German scientists of the Portable Room. Basically a box which fits over the sufferer's head, it has a room painted inside it and a window through which the Rambler looks while walking. There are curtains on the window so that if an attack comes on, the patient can sit down, draw the curtains closed and switch a little light on in the ceiling. Available at all good camping and walking shops.

Compass Neck — closely allied to Pentax Stoop, Sunset Cramp and Buttercup Back, this complaint is caused by the sufferer remaining too long in a fixed position, carrying heavy cameras, examining wildflowers *etc*. Quite painful in certain cases though rarely fatal, this complaint does claim a large number of victims.

Treatment — in most cases manipulation and massage are successful and in recent years Dr J. Perelman of the Centre

For Rambling Diseases, Stalling Busk, has been experimenting with small Japanese ladies walking barefoot all over the patient and so far has claimed a ninety-five per cent success rate.

Wet Grass Bum Rot — perhaps one of the most distressing diseases to strike at Ramblers. It is caused by repeated soakings sustained while sitting in wet grass. The chlorophyl in the grass encourages the activities of a particularly nasty mite (*Trouserus Nibblus*). The symptoms are dizziness, the sudden ability to speak Urdu and bits falling off. There is no known cure and sadly many of the sufferers die.

Prevention — carry a folding chair with you wherever you go or, if you must sit on the grass, carry a hair dryer with you.

Stings and Bites — stings and bites from insects and the like are rarely fatal in Britain and Ireland, although there are a few 'wee beasties' that can cause you problems. I will deal with them here in order of lethality.

The Yorkshire Black Widow — a deadly spider found frequently under parkin bushes. One bite from this arachnid causes loss of memory during which time the patient is unable to remember the names of Yorkshire's greatest spin bowlers. This is followed rapidly by death. Cure: none.

Cumberland Sausage Snake — so called because of its resemblance to a long, fat, linkless sausage, this pale pink snake, often found under heather, is toothless but can give fatal sucks. Cure: none.

Methodist Garter Snake — thankfully dying out now, this snake used to be frequently found in long grass and weeds behind Methodist chapels and always struck in that area known as the 'garter area'. Rarely fatal, it often attacked courting couples and produced an embarrassing rash which had to be explained away, often unsuccessfully. Cure: wear long trousers until the marks go; avoid riding a bicycle if possible since this only aggravates the condition.

The Common Wasp and Bee — there's nothing really common about the wasp and bee, particularly if one stings you. If stung by a wasp or bee you must kill it. It doesn't make the sting any less painful but it's good to get your own back on the little swines. Cure: pull out the sting and suck the poison out of the wound. If it's in a place you can't easily reach you'll soon find out who your friends are.

Midges — God didn't drive Adam and Eve out of the Garden of Eden, the midges did. For something so small midges are incredibly powerful and can cause mischief way beyond any expectation based on their size. It is said that Napoleon lost one of his most important battles because of midges.

He is said to have been waving them away so fiercely as he sat on his horse, Trigger, on the hill overlooking the

battle that his commanders interpreted his hand movements as signals and began sending their men in all directions until they were falling and tripping over each other and were easy prey for the Prussian gunners.

But the midges Napoleon came across were as nothing compared to the midges you find in Scotland. They are definitely getting their own back for Culloden.

Just as you're putting your tent up by some lovely lochside or some lonely burn, the midges arrive. The secret underground bunker where Central Midge Intelligence Scotland has its war room, picks you up on the early warning system and scrambles all the midges in your area. Out they come with claymore and dirk and within minutes you're cowering in the tent, a mass of swellings, your eyes disappearing in the pink blancmange that was your face. Millions have accompanied you into the tent. You try to smoke them out and render yourself unconscious from the fumes. You try and beat them to death in a blind rage and rip a hole in the tent with the mallet you've been using to kill them. Millions of reinforcements pile in through the breach in the canvas. Whimpering and slobbering you run, like Manfred on the Jungfrau, and leap into the water, fully clothed, lying there submerged. The only part of your anatomy above the surface is your nose and on that tens of millions of midges are making jamboree and having their dinner.

In the Middle Ages churchmen used to debate how many angels could dance on the head of a pin (well it gave them something to do on a wet Wednesday afternoon). They'd have been better off debating how many Scots midges can dine off a Rambler's nose. It would probably take several thousand IBM computers and the electricity supply of a medium-sized city to work it out and in the end the little buggers would still be there as soon as you unpacked the tent, laughing and noshing away.

Natural and Unnatural Enemies of the Rambler

The Rambler has few real enemies beyond old age and low-flying aircraft, but the ones he does have are pretty formidable and need to be taken into account by anybody contemplating anything more than a walk to the corner shop.

Thermos Beetle (Beetlus Thermosae) — of recent years the arrival of this beetle into the British Isles from Europe has caused problems of monumental dimensions. Thousands of Ramblers have been scalded near to death on unpacking the thermos from the rucksack only to have it burst before their eyes, drenching them with tea close to boiling point.

To date the beetle has few known enemies beyond the Natterjack Toad and is increasing its numbers every year. The only thing you can do is watch out for tell-tale signs such as brown spots on the outer casing of the thermos and hairline fatigue cracks in the cap. All in all, you are better off changing your thermos at least every ten years.

The Tupperware Weevil (Weevelus Alkathenus) — believed to have been brought here on a ship from America five or six years ago, this weevil recently devastated the Tupperware harvest in Batislava causing the price of raw, unrefined Tupperware to reach a world high. Crop spraying has reduced the problem to some extent but the weevil is still around and has been known to attack sandwich boxes on a fairly regular basis, particularly in the Midlands. Scientists conducting research into the weevil for the MAFF are currently working on a form of weevil-proof container into which the Tupperware can go and have so far had some success with lead and cobalt.

Dogs (Canem Nastyus) — 'He won't bite', they say, as their Pekinese sinks its yellow, rabies-infected fangs into your gluteus maximus. It's always too late to point out to them that they're wrong when you're being carted off to hospital foaming at the mouth and snapping at the ambulance man's ankles. There are two sorts of dogs, those that might bite you and those that will bite you. Any others you might come across are not dogs, they are cats in disguise.

Bulls (Cowus Testiculus) — in Britain now, following a recent Act of Parliament, it is perfectly legal for a farmer to keep a bull in a field with a public footpath running through it providing that it's a non-dairy bull. Now I don't know how good your bull recognition is, but mine's pretty hopeless. I just about know the difference between a bull

BEWARE OF THE NON DAIRY BULL

and a cow – how am I going to tell the difference between a non-dairy bull and a dairy bull? Does the dairy bull have a milk bottle painted on its side? Does it somehow look milkier? Rumour has it that the National Farmer's Union are thinking of giving out free wall charts showing all the different breeds of bull so that you can sort them out into dairy and non-dairy. Fine, providing you can do the hundred metres hurdles in 10.6 seconds with the chart in your hand. Just as there are only two kinds of dogs, so there are only two kinds of bulls, the kind that might kill you and the kind that will kill you.

Unless you're an Olympic sprinter, then you should keep out of any field with anything bigger than a hedgehog in it. If it's got horns on, it might be a bull and if it's not got horns on, it still might be a bull. There's only one way to tell if it's a bull or not and since you need to creep up close behind it to find out, that method is ruled out completely.

Bogs

A researcher at Brunel University, investigating soil types in the uplands of Britain, came up with the staggering information recently that there are several types of bogs. I could have told him that years ago but I would have added that the only difference is that they're all equally bad, if you know what I mean. The main types of bogs you need to worry about are those you can get out of and those you can't.

There's nothing funnier than watching people floundering and flummoxing their way through the first type of bog. Looking like spring-loaded hobgoblins who've been eating magic mushrooms, they hobble and leap and hop their way across the ooze, sometimes sinking in it up to their knees. Muttering and weeping, teeth grinding in a

fury of frustration, they eventually make it to the other side, covered in peaty mud and looking like freshly-painted gingerbread men as the bog snickers and plops behind them. The only things that stops you from splitting your sides laughing is the knowledge that you've got to go through it next. The second kind of bog, the sort that doesn't let you go, is the sort in which they keep finding prehistoric people like Tollund Man, perfectly preserved from head to toe. Archaeologists have for long thought that 'the bodies in the bog', as they call them, 'were put there as some sort of ritual burial'. Well, I've got news for the archaeologists. They're the bodies of lost Ramblers who ended up there when they got stuck taking a short cut back to the bus stop. If they look in their pockets they'll find a YHA membership card and a Mars bar wrapper.

Angry Farmers (Agricolus Manicus) — farmers, on the whole, are reasonable people, so that if you meet an angry one there's usually a good reason for him being angry. Perhaps someone has left his gates open, letting all his stock out into the road, perhaps his subsidy hasn't arrived, perhaps someone has trampled down his crops, perhaps a fox has killed one of his tractors or perhaps his wife has just run off with a Rambler.

In any case, there's not much you can do. If he comes towards you with a stick, run. If he comes towards you with a gun, run very fast. Shot leaves a cartridge at something like fifteen hundred miles an hour, so that you need to be able to run at fifteen hundred and one miles an hour to avoid being peppered.

Shirty Publicans (Boozus Narkus) — fairly rare in former years but recently on the increase in country pubs, this menace has managed to destroy most of the good old English pubs that sold good ale, made reasonable food, didn't charge an arm and a leg for bed and breakfast and had a domino table or skittle alley where the locals came to play a few games after work. After the ravages of this monster the pubs are carpeted and either so covered in formica that they look like a transport cafe or are done up to look as somebody imagined they looked in Elizabethan times. This usually means that they are covered in fibreglass beams, a gaslog fire burns in the centre of the room in an imitation log basket and there is so much brass and copper in the place that it looks like a cookpot shop in a Kurdish bazaar. To cap it all, the pub of the Shirty Publican is always filled with juke boxes and video games so that it looks like the flight deck of the Star Ship *Enterprise* and sounds like a nuclear submarine on full asdic alert, being piloted by Status Quo. (I actually like Status Quo very much but I like to be able to decide when I want to hear them!) Nobody wearing overalls or hiking boots is allowed in and the place is full of yuppies throwing lager down their necks.

The Shirty Publican is usually a retired ex-serviceman who thinks that anybody who doesn't want to nuke Moscow is a communist and anybody who thinks that black people are the same as white people is an anarchist about to blow up the Royal Family and rape a convent full of nuns.

He is difficult to avoid since he's usually got the only pub for miles around but he is, thankfully, easily spotted. He usually wears a cravat and cavalry twill trousers, calls everybody squire and is married to a woman who has her hair rinsed and permed four times a week, has a face like a bag full of chisels and sits at the corner of the bar getting solidly drunk and banning people from the pub at the rate of four a night. Faced with a choice between meeting a mad bull in a field full of thistles and that woman in her own pub, the bull wins every time. At least the bull admits he'd like to kill you.

Chapter Five

The Philosophy of Rambling – Existentialism and Rambling
– Sartre and Russell on the use of Crampons and Dubbin –
Locke and Hobbes on the function of the YHA within the
boundaries of Conceptual Reality – Science and Rambling –
Great Inventions in Rambling – Failed Inventions in
Rambling

'I think, therefore, I am.' When Descartes made this
statement at the bar of the Lauigngh Dyselcix,
Caughtshort in the Marsh, the landlord's wife banned him
on the spot – but not before those immortal words had
been scribbled down on a beer mat by a *Sun* journalist
who'd been following Descartes round trying to find if
there was any truth in the rumour that Descartes had been
doing rudies with the barmaid at the pub.

Short of a story, the journalist published the words in
the *Sun* next morning as a byline for the page three girl of
the day, attributing the words to her.

> *Lovely Francoise Molegelder of Wallasey isn't just a pretty
> face! Under that gorgeous curvy 42:32:38 bushel, this pert
> nineteen-year-old miss is hiding a bright brainy light. 'I think,
> therefore, I am,' says Philosophizing Françoise. And who are
> we to argue? Watch out Bertrand Russell we say!*

Descartes was furious and sued the paper. The matter
was settled out of court for an undisclosed sum and
Descartes' words became the motto of his local Rambling
club, the Mensa Dropouts and Caving and Walking Club.
'I think, therefore, I am,' they would sing in chorus as they
marched through forest glade and along Alpine path.

'You only think you are, you barmpots,' shouted angry farmers from the meadows. 'Shut that row up! You're frightening the chickens, you lot and your bloody philosophy. You can't eat philosophy can you? Where would you be if us farmers went round spouting statements like that all day, eh? Dead, that's where you'd be! Because there'd be naff all to eat!'

And poor old Descartes and the rest would wander on, discouraged and crestfallen.

If we look at the roots of philosophy, as it pertains to Rambling, we can read in the earliest philosophers attempts to reconcile concepts such as thought and existence, morals and ethics with Rambling.

Plato in his *Symposium* says, 'Fred Aeschylus went out Rambling today and ended up dead for his trouble... Bloody rum doo, life! Buggered if I can make it out. Here one minute, gone the next. Makes you wonder what it's all about. I mean there was Fred this morning eating his breakfast in the Acropolis with all the lads. "Where you

off today then Fred?" I ask him. "Just over the Elysian fields and up Olympus," he says. "Enjoy yourself," I say. "Too true I will," he says. Next thing is old SophoCleese in the pub says, "Hear about Fred then?" "What about Fred," says I. "Dead," says SophoCleese. "Leave it out," I says, "I was with him this morning." "Straight up," says SophoCleese, "I had it from Homer down at the bookies. He's crossing them fields down past the Tragedium and he meets a dairy Minotaur on the footpath. He tries to ignore it and just keeps on walking, like, so as not to get too upset but the Minotaur starts pawing the ground and ripping trees up. Old Fred starts running but you know he had that gammy leg from the Trojan war, what with being bent up inside that wooden horse with his leg under him half the night you'd have a bad cartlidge too wouldn't you."

'"Get on with it," I says. "Well that's it," says SophoCleese. "Fred's hobbling along the path, the Minotaur's after him, Fred falls over, it's Goodnight Vienna for Fred and an early lunch for the Minotaur."

'So after SophoCleese goes out I starts thinking. What a rum doo it all is. I mean there's old Aeschylus this morning pulling on his boots, not a care in the world. Next thing you know it's the wooden overcoat job and he's breakfast, dinner and tea for several hundredweight of mythological meat. It makes you think.

'I mean Fred was alive and walking about just like you and me at half past nine this morning, by half past eleven he's just a few bones and indigestion for a monster. I mean where's Fred? Where's he gone? Where's his soul gone to? The real Fred, not those bits of bone and skin and that. There's no Life in them. I mean where's Fred's *anima* gone, you know, his spirit wotsit – his soul? I mean there must be some purpose in it all. We can't just die and that's it!

'And where do we come from in the first place? That's

another thing. All these people that's been alive since the beginnings of Time. Where did they all come from? All them individuals. Takes a bit of thinking about that does. Anyway my brain hurts now. I'm off to the pub. But it's a rum doo.'

The Rum Doo School of Philosophy, founded in Ancient Greece by Plato, had a tremendous influence on the Mediterranean world. SophoCleese was so influenced by Plato's Rum Doo philosophy when he heard it in the pub that night that he bought a notebook from Athens Woolworths and went straight home and wrote a very depressing play about a man who marries his own mother and then gets so upset about it he pokes his own eyes out. In fact the whole of Athens was very depressed by this Rum Doo school of thought and went round with very long faces indeed, upsetting all the tourists who were not used to this kind of thing at all. There they'd come, all those miles on the DanAir Trireme, expecting bazouki music, kebabs and retsina wine and all they got was bad service, frozen chips and people walking round shaking their heads muttering, 'It's a rum doo and no mistake.'

In fact, if it hadn't been for Archy Medes overfilling his bath so that when he got in and sat himself down, he flooded the bathroom, fusing all the lights in town, giving everybody something to laugh at, they'd still all be wobbling round Athens with their chins trailing in the dust, sighing heavily and banging their heads on the Doric columns in sheer frustration at the misery of it all.

After Plato, nobody did much thinking for quite some time since they found it all too depressing, so philosophy suffered a tremendous loss in popularity and was replaced at parties by games like Postman's Knock and Charades, until the Middle Ages.

In the Middle Ages, philosophy came back into fashion and, as I mentioned before, people at fashionable dinner parties stayed up all night arguing about how many angels could dance on the head of a pin, which was a bit stupid anyway since nobody in their right mind is going to hold a disco on a pin.

An other thing they were concerned about was whether there really is a God and if not why can't we all break out of here?

It was the Scholastic Philosophers and Alchemists of the Middle Ages who tried to work out ways of turning base metal into gold. Nowadays we'd call them forgers and they'd get locked up, but philosophers could get away with murder in those days. Mind you, nowadays they call themselves professors and get jobs running departments at universities and sit round all day talking about the meaning of meaning and whether there really is an ultimate truth and doing 'research' into philosophy. Some of them even talk about the Philosophy of mathematics. How can you have a philosophy of mathematics? One and one added together make two, and three into nine goes three times and anybody who tells you any different is a meringue.

I once met a mathematical philosopher in a Cotswold pub, when I was walking round there.

'Ah,' he said. 'But suppose there was a case where one added to one didn't make two but made three.'

'Suppose you get your hand in your pocket and buy a pint,' I said, realizing I was in the company of a madman.

'But can't you see the beauty of numbers?' he said, ordering a packet of pork scratchings and offering the barmaid the wrong money.

'Not when there's a lot of them and they're on the electricity bill,' I answered, reaching for my pint.

'But don't you think there's an essential beauty in the fact that the square root of minus one is minus point three three three three recurring on into infinity?'

I stared at a fly that was crawling across the chest of the denim-clad girl on the Big D Peanuts dispenser.

'Given that minus one is a concept used to facilitate equations and has no existence in what we term "the real world", I am not going to lose any sleep worrying about the square root of bugger all.'

'You're an intellectual Luddite,' he hissed and with that turned on his heel and stormed towards the door, falling over the landlord's dog on the way. The dog bit him.

Bertrand Russell ended up in a similar argument with Sartre in a pub called The Gerbil and Harpsichord in Heckmondwyke. They'd been walking in the Pennines and were waiting for Françoise Sagan to turn up in the car and take them home. They'd had a few pints and were talking to some of the old colliers, playing dominoes by the fire, about the role of the syllogism in symbolic logic. Sartre became very agitated when one of the old blokes started quoted Wittgenstein on the function of structure within linguistic codes.

'*C'est tout mon derrière,*' shouted Sartre, banging the table, knocking his spring onion flavoured crisps on to the floor. Then, realizing that the old man didn't speak French, he stated his argument again in broken English. 'Eet is all my berm, my friend. Wittgenstein 'ad absolutement no understanding of ze problems. Ee saw langwage as a system of codes zat could be analized like mathematic and ee ignore zee emotions zat go wiz certaine words like Death, Life and Birth!'

'Aye! Yon frog's reet tha knows, Albert,' interrupted another old collier. 'Wittgenstein were a reet wart. Tha wouldn't get me dahn t'pit ageean with 'im. We were goin' dahn Grimey Pit wun day in t'cage an Wittgenstein turns to ma an sez, "Dust tha know ah've forgotten me snap*." "Well yer a pillock," I told him, "an' yer gettin' none of mine." He were a reet gobbin were Wittgenstein.'

'It's all very well talking about Language,' said

---

* *Snap* — food and drink carried to work by colliers in South Yorkshire.

Bertrand Russell, 'but language is only a tool of reasoning and a very imperfect tool too. What you've got to do is come back to pure thought and ask yourself the purely fundamental questions of existence. For example, are we really here or do we just imagine we're here?'

'Well when I get 'ome terneet and our lass starts givin' me 'ot tongue and cold shoulder fer bein in t'pub, ah'll tell 'er ah weren't 'ere ah only thowt ah were. Bye that's a bloody good un that is. Ah'll lie in bed termorrer an ah waint go dahn t'pit, ah'll imagine ah'mn gooin dahn. Then come Friday when ah goo fer me wages they'll tell me ter imagine ah've got um.'

'Look at it this way,' said Russell. 'Do you see that pint on the table there?'

'Aye,' said the collier, 'course ah do. Ah just bowt it.'

'Well, how do you know it really exists?' asked Russell.

'Cos ah just paid sixty-two bloody pence for it,' shouted the collier, 'an ah wunt pay sixty-two pence fer summat that weren't there, would ah, yer great wazzock!'

'So you believe in the absolute existence of all matter?' asked Russell, sensing victory.

'Nay. Ah just know that bloody pint's on t' table.'

'Ah but that's only because your senses tell you it's there. To a deaf man music has no existence, to a blind man there is no such thing as light. If you were to close your eyes how would you know that that pint is still there?'

'Because if it isn't I'll smack yer in't gob. Comin' up 'ere with yer fancy bloody London talk. We 'ad people like you drivin' buses in t' General Strike. I've a good mind ter punch yer 'ed in. You and yer conceptual reality. I 'appen to be chairman of the Heckmondwyke Hedonists Existentialists and Pigeon Fanciers Club so you can bugger off back to London and take that frog with you!'

Sensing that things were turning nasty, the two philosophers hurriedly left the pub and waited for Françoise Sagan in the car park.

The major contribution made by Russell and Sartre to Rambling was the work they did on the development of dubbin for wet-weather walking and crampons for snow and ice work.

Sartre invented crampons during a climbing holiday in the Alps, when he discovered that if he held toothpicks between the toes of his bare feet he was able to ascend quite steep ice slopes. It was a short step from that to hammering them into his boot and wasn't long before he'd

137

designed a strap-on set of toothpicks that could be fastened
on to the bottom of the boots. Borrowing Trotsky's ice
pick he ascended the Matterhorn in grand style.

Meanwhile, back in England, Russell made the first
dubbin-aided ascent of Mam Tor in a rainstorm and
reported only minor trench foot, a breakthrough in foul-
weather walking. His attempt to use dubbin to waterproof
sandwiches, however, was a total disaster and got him
thrown out of the Happy Academics Rambling Club.

The influence of Eastern Philosophy on Rambling can
hardly be over-emphasized. In his book, *Zen and the Art of
Bull Recognition*, the American author, J. P. Frogwalloper,
looks at the Buddhist approach to Rambling.

The book is written as the personal account of the
journey of a man in search of his soul. His journey takes
him away from the city and out into the mountains, where
the teachings of Buddha are brought home to him when he

is shot at by a hunter who thinks he is the Yeti, taught to yodel by a nun with a thumbscrew and suffers a fractured skull when a seven-pound beech nut falls on his head.

'To know peace that passeth all understanding,' he writes, 'I meditated each morning for four hours while lying naked in a bed of thorns and stinging nettles. The sheep came and laughed at me, rolling on their backs with their legs in the air, but I ignored them for I knew that it is only by subduing the body that we can liberate the soul. When the snows came I went out naked into snow drifts and sat for hours contemplating the Buddha, the All Knowing One. Then bits of me started falling off and I thought to myself, "This Buddha's a right pillock" and I walked down from the mountains and had a Chicken Rogan Josh and a pint of lager in the Taj Mahal Restaurant near the Town Hall and felt a lot better for it.'

He eventually finds his soul drinking alone in a late bar in one of the seedier parts of town and manages to get it to come back home with him by promising to give it its own dress allowance and generally to take better care of it in future.

In recent years, Rambling philosophers have begun to turn away from the atheistic doctrine of uncertainty promulgated by the laid-back French Rambler, Tooloose Tootrek, and are beginning to look again at the concept of God as an all-knowing infinite omnipotent being. Rumour has it that he was seen on Coniston Old Man by some Born Again Ramblers but as yet there is no proof of this.

'We turned over a stone,' the *Westmoreland Gazette* quoted one of the walkers as saying, 'and there he was, a little old man with a grey beard and a tee-shirt on, that said "I am Omnipotent." So I said to my mate Tone d'you think it's Him? If it is, said Tone, make him do us a miracle. Go on, I said, do us a miracle. Naff off, said the

Old Geezer. Who do you think I am? So I dropped the stone back on him. But I still think it was God. Anyway, it'll be something to tell the grandchildren, won't it?'

Rambling and Science

Ever since the day that primitive Man left his cave with his stick and a bag of dinosaur bones to gnaw on and set off on a ramble round Stonehenge, Man has sought to improve the quality of his walking by the application of the scientific method. After the first Ramblers discovered that their feet wore out on long Rambles, the first boots were

invented. These were of Tyrannosaurus Rex hide and were very tough. They were also very expensive since tyrannosaurus hides were very hard to get hold of and the number of prehistoric cobblers who ended up a bit dead trying to persuade the great lizards to part with enough skin for six pairs of size nine hiking boots was astronomical. A substitute was eventually discovered when a Stone Age mum left the porridge pot on too long and her husband discovered that by dipping his feet into the cooling mess he was able to coat them with a hard-wearing and flexible instant boot which would last for up to fifty miles before it needed renewing and which he could also eat if he got hungry.

Hard on the heels of the boot came the invention of walking breeches, which were invented soon after the invention of barbed wire in the early Middle Ages. Barbed wire was invented by a nun of the Order of the Little Sisters of the Not Badly Off, to keep the nuns in and the men out of the convent. A Nasturtium Monk, called Brother Canus Pearadime, saw the barbed wire, thought it was a good idea, took out a worldwide patent on it and changed his name to Rothschild.

Barbed wire began to appear everywhere as landowners and robber barons fenced in the land and blocked off footpaths. Many a Rambler wobbling along in nothing but the skirt which was standard wear for men in those days, discovered to his cost the price that could be paid for hurdling a barbed wire fence too low. It wasn't long before they began petitioning the Mediaeval Guild of Garment Makers for something more substantial and the trouser was invented. Special Rambling trousers with double thickness lead-lined crotches were soon available in the stores and the 'Barbed Wire Yodel' became a thing of the past – almost.

The map was invented when people began to get fed up with giving long verbal instructions. A day's Ramble, prior to the invention of maps, could take hours to describe and you'd have to remember all the instructions very carefully otherwise bits of you would be found *etc.*, *etc.*

People used to fall out like mad in those days and would argue for ages about the route.

'He said go left at the gibbet and right at the whipping block then left by the leper hospital, round the ducking stool and on up past the leech gatherer's, through the teazle field and past the hurdle maker's.'

'He did heck as like. He said go right at the gibbet and up past the pinfold then up past that hovel where old Lear was squatting before his daughters turfed him out, turn left at the tree where the jester hanged himself and up Pillycock Hill. You want to keep your ears open you do!'

The invention of the map stopped most of this sort of arguing and saved a lot of marriages. Instead people began to argue not about where they were going but where they were.

'Are you sure we're here?'

'Course I'm sure.'

'Well, there's no lake here. We should have been at Wastwater by now.'

'It's probably just around the corner. Hang on, I'll ask this bloke on the camel.'

The compass was invented after it was discovered that people who didn't live in an area had trouble knowing which way up a map was supposed to go, a point that was made most forcibly when two hundred ramblers walked into the sea and drowned at Land's End after setting off for John O'Groats. Jumbo Frogmorton, a blacksmith in Chipping Sodbury, invented the compass when he discovered that hammering a piece of metal made it magnetic. He discovered this one day when the anvil on which he was hammering a horseshoe swung round to face North and fell on his toes.

When news of his discovery spread, people began walking everywhere with anvils tied round their necks. It was only after it was discovered that any piece of metal would do that mediaeval doctors were able to sleep at nights instead of having to answer the doorbell every ten minutes to another Rambler with a double hernia.

The bog stilt was invented by Hiram Loveday, an American inventor who, in Victorian times, also invented the underwear-proof compass. Bog stilts were a very useful invention in their time. When folded down they measured eleven inches and were fitted into two leather holsters that could be slung on the belt, and when extended they enabled the user to cross all but the deepest of bogs. They fell out of favour in the early years of this century after the introduction of the portable bog bridge. The underwear-proof compass was invented for use on long Rambles after it was discovered that underwear worn for a long time becomes magnetic and can attract a compass needle towards it. This was only discovered after thousands of walkers on the Pennine Way had spent days walking round and round in circles near Malham bumping into each other saying, 'Didn't we see you in Malham,' for days until it dawned on them what was happening. The invention of the underwear-proof compass, sheathed in its lead-lined box, was a great boon to the long distance Rambler.

A number of inventions that were produced to make Rambling safer or more enjoyable failed to catch the walking public's imagination. One of these was Bull Repellent. Hailed as a foolproof aerosol spray bull

deterrent, it was supposed to be a chemical spray compound which made the wearer smell like another bull, thus frightening off any bull the wearer might come across. The manufacturers had, however, overlooked the fact that something like ten per cent of the world bull population is gay. This lack of foresight had disastrous results and many thousands of Ramblers were forced to run for their lives as amorous bulls advanced towards them, obviously intent on something other than murder.

The folding cardboard portaloo was another rambling disaster. Hailed as a particular boon for lady Ramblers, it proved to be more of an embarrassment. They were prone to collapse and blew away easily in anything other than the mildest breeze. When wet, the gum that held them together, softened and the sides often sprang apart leaving the user exposed to all eyes. In heavy persistent rain they went soggy and draped themselves round the user like a

shroud. All in all, several thousand Ramblers got their money back, but not before there had been many nervous breakdowns and several suicides.

The Rucksack

Prior to the invention of the rucksack, people had gorged themselves silly before setting off on a Ramble, hoping to be able to live off the stored energy for as long as it took. This was not always successful and many thousands of people died on things like the Crusades which were long Rambles to the Holy Land in search of relics and Arabs to bash. Then a mediaeval knight, Sir Tainly Knott, who was in the Holy Land on a business trip (he was in the relic-exporting and Arab-bashing business) saw a camel drinking water at an oasis. Amazed at the amount of water the camel was drinking, the knight asked a passing rif how this might be. Told that the camel stored gallons of water in its hump, the knight was forcibly struck with an idea and on his return to England tried to get his invention off the ground. Unfortunately it failed miserably when people refused to have humps sewn on their backs.

It was another seven hundred years before Adolphe Sax, the inventor of the bags they bring coal in, invented the rucksack as a carrying case for the newly invented phone.

Endword

Whither Rambling?

If we look back at the world of the early Ramblers, Moses and the Kosher Ramblers, the Brigham Young Mormon Rambling Club and the Jumbo Rambling Club it all seems so simple and so innocent. Today we live in a far different world. All Moses had to worry about was plagues of frogs and his walking stick biting him. The modern Rambler has all the perils of the modern world to contend with.

Acid rain can strip the clothes from a Rambler in 12.5 seconds and Ramblers walking in West Cumbria have been known to glow in the dark and grow two heads. We are facing dangers never faced before in the world of Rambling. The pro-nuclear lobby tell us that radiation is harmless and if anybody dies of cancer they must have caught it off a lavatory seat and yet a Rambler walking along the beach near Sellafield (alias Windscale) recently was kicked to death by a six-foot luminous prawn.

Have you noticed, by the way, how it's perfectly reasonable and fine for BNFL to change the name of their festering pile and yet if you or I changed our names the police would be round kicking the door down accusing us of being international terrorists?

Great areas of Britain are now in the hands of the military and are used as training areas and firing ranges. Providing you can run faster than a Howitzer shell this need not bother you. Any unexploded shells on the footpath can easily be dealt with the aid of a metal detector (available at any good ex-Army store) and with the manual *Unexploded Shells, Anti-Personnel Mines and Nuclear Missiles — Defusing Procedures — Ministry of Defence Pamphlet. WDXB 4567 MNB 90K.*

Terrorism on footpaths is yet another problem that the modern Rambler has to take into account whenever he steps out of his front door. The hijacking of the summit of Ben Nevis by a group claiming to be Members of the Yorkshire Separatist Popular Front is a perfect example of this. If it had not been for the speedy intervention of a crack group of Girl Guides who were doing their Pet Care and Anti-Terrorist Badge on that very peak at the time, the fourteen lady weightlifters of the Sappho Rambling Club might be there still.

Competition has started to creep into the climbing world with thousands of people turning out to watch crag rats climbing against the clock on rock faces in France and Britain. How long will it be before Rambling becomes a competitive sport like climbing or ballroom dancing? It makes my blood run cold to think that in the near future the BBC may be running a series called 'Come Rambling', compered by Terry Wogan.

And coming on to the field now are the Eric and Doris Scroat Formation Ramblers from Surbiton. Last year they came a close second to José Arriva and his Latin American Ramblers. This year they're hoping for great things. For those of you with black and white tellies or even funny colour ones, the ladies are wearing salmon pink satin shorts, edged with lavender coloured lace. Their blouses are primrose yellow, again in satin and edged with flounces of tulle. Their socks are a lovely shade of purple and the whole outfit is set off with bright orange fell boots. The men are wearing cream satin shorts, red cummerbunds and leaf green corduroy shorts with reinforced gussets. Their socks are a stunning red and their boots a bright sky blue.

Their first Ramble is an Old Fashioned Wander and the music they've chosen for it is the Ivy Benson Band playing South of the Border.

The mind boggles.

In today's world it is the fringe element in our society that seems to attract the most attention and in recent years the fringes of the Rambling world have included people like Screw Loose O' Trek, the Impressionist Rambler who invented Disco Rambling and Display Rambling. Members of his Red Rucksack Display Rambling Team appear regularly at agricultural shows and galas rambling through hoops of fire, rambling over twenty parked double decker buses and leave the show field rambling in pyramid fashion standing on each other's shoulders.

The Sealed Knot Society dress up as Roundheads and Cavaliers and re-enact some of the great battles of the English Civil War. How long will it be before people are dressing up as Hell's Ramblers and Ladies from the Bath Townswomen's Guild are re-enacting the famous Battle of Wookey Hole Tea-Rooms when seventeen Hell's Ramblers were taken to hospital with umbrella jabs and

hatpin scratches.

Like all things, Rambling, in moderation, is a good thing. Some people, however, have never heard the old dictum, 'You can have too much of a good thing' and sadly, of recent years, there has been an increase in the number of people to whom Rambling has become an addiction worse than any drug or alcohol.

Homes have been broken and families split by this most terrible of afflictions. The victims, or Rambolics as they are known to doctors, spend every waking moment out Rambling. Secretly and furtively they will sneak from the house telling their wives or husbands that they are going to the aero-modelling club or ladies' squash night. Then, having changed into their Rambling gear in the coal shed, they will jump on the bus and head for open country, going missing for hours.

Later they return shamefaced to the bosoms of their families, crying and repentent, vowing never to do it again. But they do it again and again until their families crack under the strain or they themselves end up sleeping rough under the arches together with all the other social derelicts that our modern world creates.

Thankfully, there is an organization now which can help these poor wretches. Ramblers Anonymous, a spin-off from Teetotalers Anonymous, holds meetings in most major cities almost any night of the week. You can find their number in the phone book. Weaning the addict from his dependence is a slow and painful process. Sufferers sit round discussing their various life histories and the weakness that drove them to this terrible addiction.

Medical centres have been established to treat acute Rambolics in some of our hospitals and treatment is usually one of two kinds. A gradual weaning process aims at turning the patient away from dependence while a second method, developed by doctors at Cambridge University, first throws the patient into cold turkey when he or she is kept in a locked room for twenty-four hours with nothing in the room but a pair of boots. This is followed by a course of avoidance therapy. The patient is shown slides in a darkened room that are alternately of the Lake District or Dartmoor, and of Birmingham Bull Ring and Milton Keynes. Every time the slides of the countryside are flashed up the patient receives an electric shock and every time the grotty bits are shown the patient is given a Good Boy Doggy Choc. The treatment has so far proved successful in ninety-three per cent of cases.

I mentioned the dangers of competition Rambling before but another more insidious, and perhaps ultimately more dangerous, threat has crept into the Rambling world over the last few years. This is opportunism and commercialism in the shape of Ramblergrams and Nude Rambling. Both are transatlantic imports into our society and for them we have to thank that freak religionist, head pastor of The Church of People Over Sixty in California Who Have a Lot of Money and are Going to Die Soon and Leave it to Me, creator of the ultimate in bad taste, the Wet Tee-shirt Granny Competition, Hiram J. Rippemof.

Nude Rambling is fast catching on in the South where

the weather is warmer and although it has not yet taken a hold in the far North the signs are that, like a plague, it is spreading its tentacles ever onwards. Deaths from exposure and severe nettling have occurred and medical health chiefs in several counties are said to be alarmed at the increase in diseases such as Stile Splinter and Warble Fly among nude Ramblers.

The Ramblergram is pure crass commercialism and would be laughable were it not an embarrassment. People knocking at your door, dressed as Ramblers, singing Happy Birthday to the tune of I Love To Go A-wandering, is not my idea of fun.

Of recent years sponsorship has begun to creep into Rambling and on the hills now on any Sunday afternoon you can see people sporting cagoules and tee-shirts advertising their sponsors' products. Slogans saying 'EAT AT THE COPPER KETTLE' and 'SCOTT'S ANTARC-TIC COLD CREAM FOR CHAPPED THIGHS' are bad enough, but only last week on the summit of Snowdon I saw a tee-shirt with an advert for a proprietary brand of contraceptive condom being sported on the chest of a young lady from Barnsley. Now surely that is taking things too far!

Condom, by the way, has always struck me as a funny word. I don't know why it is really. I somehow imagine a judge in court putting on the black cap and in a serious voice saying to the guilty party, 'I have no alternative but to condom you to death!'

So whither Rambling?

One of the greatest events in the history of Rambling, and one whose impact we are only just beginning to assess, took place when the Russian astronaut Colonel Lemonkurd Leonid became the first man to go walkabout in space.

Does the future then hold its hand out to us to lead us forward and away to the stars? How long will it be before the shape of things to come leads us out to Ramble in the vast, never ending, limitless, so to speak, infinities of outer space?

The imagination and the dreams of Man know no limits, on and ever on he has always searched and must ever search, for it is within his very nature like the beating of his heart and the surging of his blood and like the tendency to get chincough from sitting on cold steps. And let those of you who are afraid of Progress remember that the mind that gave us germ warfare, Agent Orange and the Atom Bomb, also gave us Coca Cola, frozen chips and *Daily Mirror* Bingo.

Progress will lead us then, in time, out to the stars, to the first Lunar Youth Hostel, to a little tea-room on Mars that sells genuine Martian crafts, model craters, paperweights that are Martian rocks embedded in clear plastic and earrings made from genuine Swartblaster horn and where you can get a cup of tea that doesn't cost the earth. So, as is the nature of things, Progress will lead us on to guided walking tours of far galaxies, backpacking holidays among the hills of distant planets. Perhaps, as is also the nature of things, it will lead us also to UFOs and aliens on the footpath as we wander through the mists of infinity amongst the milky moons of the planet Narkon.

'Ronald, there's a funny green thing with four eyes and big teeth in the crater in front of us.'
'Has it got horns?'
'I can't see, my torch isn't working properly.'
'Has it got any things hanging down?'
'What do you mean Ron, things?'
'You know, wotzits. That thing that killed Fred and Ethel on

Mars last year had things hanging down. Non-dairy it was too, they're not supposed to kill you that sort.'

'I think it has got things. Oh Ron, it's coming towards us. It's pawing the ground. Oh Ron, it's shaking both its heads at us! Ron, I'm frightened. It looks angry. What are we going to do, Ron?'

'You distract it while I get away, love.'

'Shouldn't it be the other way round, Ron? Shouldn't you distract it while I get away?'

'What do you think I am, barmy?'

Postscript

I thought long and hard about how to end this book and it hasn't been easy. I mean, if it was a novel it would be a piece of cake and I'd just have to write something like, 'So he shot her. The end' or 'So Noddy jumped in his little car and drove off into the sunset leaving the naughty golliwogs far behind. The end', but with a book like this it's a lot harder. There's no story, so there's no real end if you know what I mean. Anyway, I've made one up. Here it is:

Laughing, she flung herself down on the grass, her eyes wide and bright, her wet mouth beckoning him on. Her breasts under the thin cotton of her dress rose and fell softly with her breathing. Bees were murmuring in the afternoon sun. Around them the grass shimmered gently in the warm summer breezes.

'Take me,' she whispered fiercely.

'Where?' he asked, looking around him. 'I thought you liked it here.'